Scientist Church of Christ

Christian Science Hymnal

A Selection of Spiritual Songs

Scientist Church of Christ

Christian Science Hymnal
A Selection of Spiritual Songs

ISBN/EAN: 9783337083496

Printed in Europe, USA, Canada, Australia, Japan

Cover: Foto ©Thomas Meinert / pixelio.de

More available books at **www.hansebooks.com**

CHRISTIAN SCIENCE HYMNAL

A SELECTION OF

SPIRITUAL SONGS

PUBLISHED BY
CHRISTIAN SCIENCE PUBLISHING SOCIETY
BOSTON, MASS.
1893

PREFACE.

In presenting this Hymnal for the use of Christian Scientists the Committee do not claim that it is strictly scientific, as they were obliged to select very largely from hymns composed by those who were unacquainted with the teachings of Christian Science.

While not entirely composed of hymns written exactly in accordance with the doctrines of Christian Science it presents the acme of religious and poetic thought contained in the best hymns of the day, as well as in the best compositions thus far contributed by Christian Scientists.

A few Sabbath School hymns have been added to the list, without any attempt at revision, believing that for some they will meet a present need.

Much labor has been bestowed upon this compilation, by the Committee; and, in the musical department of this work, great credit is due Mr. Lyman Brackett of Boston, Mass., for untiring effort to present the most useful and varied collection of tunes ever issued in one hymnal, — the purpose being to appeal to every lover of church music, of whatever taste or ability.

Special attention has been given to the wedding of words and music, not only as to character of composition, but in respect to proper accentuation, etc., wherever it has been found possible.

The system of arrangement is original and unique. On the pages with the hymns, have been placed standard tunes familiar to every church-goer. Every second tune is by an English or German composer of unquestioned musical ability, and will be found adapted either to chorus-choir, or advanced congregational singing. Every third tune has been composed by Mr. Brackett especially for this work; and, permission from him should be secured by any person or persons desiring to use the same. Although designed particularly for quartette or choir use, many of them may be sung by the average congregation, and will be found available for responses, offertories or sentences. A few tunes have been arranged for male voices, as it is believed that there is a demand for these in some churches.

Acknowledgments are due to James McGranahan, E. O. Excel, Fillmore Bros., Mrs. W. F. Sherwin, and others for granting the use of their hymns and tunes; and to the following for the use of hymns published by them: Oliver Ditson Co., C. H. Richards, The Century Co., American Unitarian Association, Methodist Book Concern, Anson D. F. Randolph & Co., A. S. Barnes & Co., J. & A. McMillan, and others.

Boston, Mass., 1892.

CHRISTIAN SCIENCE HYMNAL

Old Hundred. L. M.

GUILLAUME FRANCK.

1

1
From all that dwell below the skies,
Let the Creator's praise arise;
Let the Redeemer's name be sung
Through every land, by every tongue.

2
Eternal are Thy mercies, Lord;
Eternal truth attends Thy word;
Thy praise shall sound from shore to shore,
Till suns shall rise and set no more.

ISAAC WATTS. *alt.*

2

1
I praise Thee, Lord, for blessings sent
To break the dream of human power.
For now my shallow cistern's spent,
I find Thy fount and thirst no more.

2
I take Thy hand and fears grow still;
Behold Thy face, and doubts remove;
Who would not yield his wavering will
To perfect truth and boundless love!

3
That truth gives promise of a dawn,
Beneath whose light I am to see,
When all these blinding vails are drawn,
This was the wisest path for me.

SECOND TUNE. L. M.

ANCIENT.

THIRD TUNE. L. M.

Missionary Chant. L. M.

CHARLES ZEUNER.

3
1
O Life that maketh all things new,—
The blooming earth, the thoughts of men!
Our pilgrim feet, wet with thy dew,
In gladness hither turn again.

2
From hand to hand the greeting flows,
From eye to eye the signals run,
From heart to heart the bright hope glows;
The seekers of the Light are one.

3
One in the freedom of the truth,
One in the joy of paths untrod,
One in the heart's perennial youth,
One in the larger thought of God;—

4
The freer step, the fuller breath,
The wide horizon's grander view,
The sense of Life that knows no death,—
The Life that maketh all things new.
SAMUEL LONGFELLOW.

4
1
Press on, press on! ye sons of light,
Untiring in your holy fight,
Still treading each temptation down,
And battling for a brighter crown.

2
Press on, press on! still look in faith
To him who conquereth sin and death :
Then shall ye hear his word, "Well done."
True to the last, press on, press on!
WILLIAM GASKELL.

SECOND TUNE. L. M.

William Henry Monk, Mus Doc.

THIRD TUNE. L. M.

SECOND TUNE. L. M.

SAMUEL WEBB.

THIRD TUNE. L. M.

Germany. L. M.

BEETHOVEN.

7

1
Jesus, what precept is like thine,
"Forgive, as ye would be forgiven!"
If heeded, O what power divine
Would then transform our earth to heaven.

2
Not by the harsh or scornful word,
Should we our brother seek to gain;
Not by the prison or the sword,
The shackle, or the clanking chain.

3
But from our hearts must ever flow
A love that will his wrong outweigh;
Our lips must only blessings know,
And wrath, and sin shall die away.

Mrs. LIVERMORE. *Abr.*

8

1
Sun of our life, Thy quickening ray
Sheds on our path the glow of day;
Star of our hope, Thy softened light
Cheers the long watches of the night.

2
Lord of all life, below, above,
Whose light is truth, whose warmth is love,
Before Thy ever-blazing throne
We ask no lustre of our own.

3
Grant us Thy truth to make us free,
And kindling hearts that burn for Thee,
Till all Thy living altars claim
One holy light, one heavenly flame!

OLIVER WENDELL HOLMES. *Abr.*

SECOND TUNE. L. M.

Henry Smart.

THIRD TUNE. L. M.

Ware. L. M.

Geo. Kingsley.

9

1
Our God shall reign where'er the sun
Does his successive journeys run;
His kingdom stretch from shore to shore,
Till moons shall wax and wane no more.

2
People and realms of every tongue
Dwell on His love with sweetest song,
And infant voices shall proclaim
Their early blessings on His name.

3
Blessings abound where'er He reigns;
The prisoner leaps to loose his chains,
The weary find eternal rest,
And all the sons of want are blest.

4
Let every creature rise, and bring
Peculiar honors to our King;
Angels descend with songs again,
And earth repeat the long Amen.

Isaac Watts.

10

1
Father, Thou Joy of loving hearts,
Thou Fount of life! Thou Light of men!
From the best bliss that earth imparts,
We turn unfilled to Thee again.

2
Thy truth unchanged hath ever stood;
Thou savest those that on Thee call;
To them that seek Thee Thou art good,
To them that find Thee, All in All.

Ray Palmer, *tr.*

SECOND TUNE. L. M.

Ancient.

THIRD TUNE. L. M.

All Saints. L. M.

W. Knapp.

11

1
Why search the future and the past?
  Why do ye look with tearful eyes,
And seek, far off, for Paradise?
  Beneath thy feet, Life's pearl is cast.

2
As deathless as His Spirit free,
  The Perfect lives and works to-day,—
As in the ancient Prophet's lay,
  Where there's an open eye to see.

3
Of all that was and is to come,
  The present holds the Mind and Cause;
And God lives in eternal laws,
  And here, to-day, upholds His throne.

4
Then rise and greet the signs that prove
  Unreal the ages' long lament!
The "one far-off divine event"
  Is *now*, and that event is Love.

Charles H. Barlow.

12

1
Lord, may Thy truth upon the heart
Now fall and dwell as heavenly dew,
And flowers of grace in freshness start
Where once the weeds of error grew!

2
May prayer now lift her sacred wings,
Contented with that aim alone
Which bears her to the King of kings,
And rests her at His sheltering throne!

Caroline Gilman.

CHRISTIAN SCIENCE HYMNAL.

SECOND TUNE. L. M.
GERMAN.

THIRD TUNE. L. M.

* The small notes are to be sung, but much softer than the large ones.

Park Street. L. M.

FREDERICK MARC ANTOINE VENUA.

13

1
Fight the good fight with all thy might,
Christ is thy strength, and Christ thy right;
Lay hold on life, and it shall be
Thy joy and crown eternally.

2
Run the straight race through God's good grace,
Lift up thine eyes, and seek His face;
Life with its way before us lies,
Christ is the path, and Christ the prize.

3
Faint not nor fear, His arms are near,
He changeth not, and thou art dear:
Rely on Him, and thou shalt see
That Christ is all in all to thee.

Rev. JOHN SAMUEL BEWLEY MONSELL. *Abr. and Alt.*

14

1
Had I the tongues of Greeks and Jews,
And nobler speech than angels use,
If love be absent, I am found
Like tinkling brass, an empty sound.

2
Should I distribute all my store
To feed the hungry, clothe the poor;
Or give my body to the flame,
To gain a martyr's glorious name:—

3
If love to God and love to men
Be absent, all my hopes are vain;
Nor tongues, nor gifts, nor fiery zeal,
The work of love can e'er fulfill.

I. WATTS. *Abr.*

SECOND TUNE. L. M.

Rt. Rev. Bishop Thomas Tuxton.

THIRD TUNE. L. M.

Zephyr. L. M.

W. B. BRADBURY.

15

1
Upon the Gospel's sacred page
 The gathered beams of ages shine;
And, as it hastens, every age
 But makes its brightness more divine.

2
On mightier wing, in loftier flight,
 From year to year does knowledge soar;
And, as it soars, the Gospel light
 Becomes effulgent more and more.

3
More glorious still, as centuries roll,
 New regions blest, new powers unfurled,
So Truth reveals the perfect whole,
 Its radiance shall o'erflow the world,—

4
Flow to restore, but not destroy;
 As when the cloudless lamp of day
Pours out its floods of light and joy,
 And sweeps the lingering mist away.
J. BOWRING. *Alt.*

16

1
Hath not thy heart within thee burned
 At evening's calm and holy hour,
As if its inmost depths discerned
 The presence of a loftier power?

2
It was the voice of God that spake
 In silence to thy silent heart;
And bade each worthier thought awake,
 And every dream of earth depart.
STEPHEN G. BULFINCH. *Abr.*

SECOND TUNE. L. M.

Rev. J. B. Dykes, Mus. Doc.

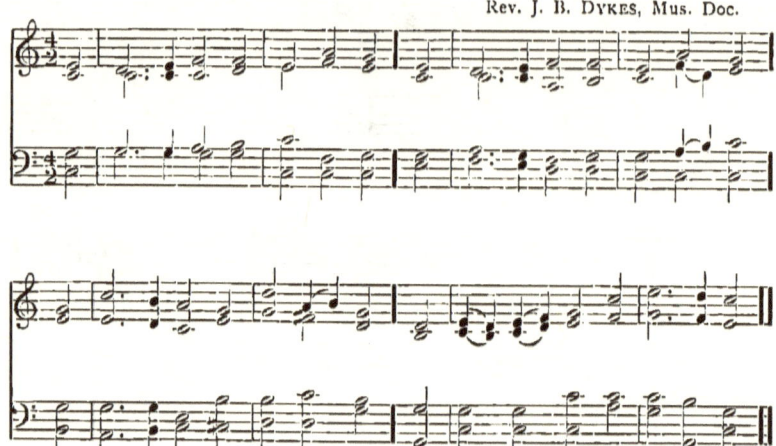

THIRD TUNE. L. M.

Woodworth. L. M.

W. B. Bradbury.

17

1
Oh, sometimes gleams upon our sight,
Through present wrong, the eternal Right;
And step by step, since time began,
We see the steady gain of man.

2
That all of good the past hath had
Remains to make our own time glad,
Our common, daily life divine,
And every land a Palestine.

3
Through the harsh noises of our day,
A low, sweet prelude finds its way;
Through clouds of doubt, and creeds of fear,
A light is breaking calm and clear.

4
Henceforth my heart shall sigh no more
For olden time and holier shore;
God's love and blessing, then and there,
Are now and here and everywhere.

J. G. Whittier.

18

1
Abide not in the realm of dreams,
O man, however fair it seems;
But with clear eye the present scan,
And hear the call of God and man.

2
Think not in sleep to fold thy hands,
Forgetful of thy Lord's commands:
From duty's claims no life is free,—
Behold, to-day hath need of thee!

William H. Burleigh.

SECOND TUNE. L. M.

ANCIENT GERMAN.

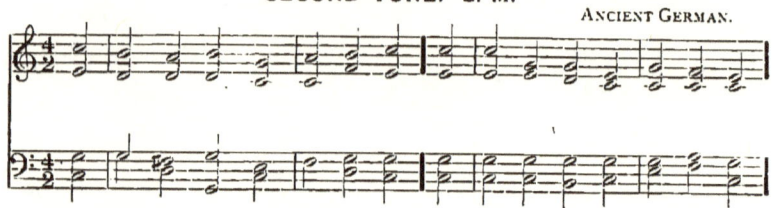

THIRD TUNE. L. M.

The small notes are for accompaniment only.

Retreat. L. M.

THOMAS HASTINGS.

19

1
When like a stranger on our sphere
The lowly Jesus wandered here,
Where'er he went affliction fled,
The sick were healed, the hungry fed.

2
With bounding steps the halt and lame,
To hail their great Deliverer, came;
For him the grave could hold no dread,
He spoke the word and raised the dead.

3
Through paths of loving-kindness led
Where Jesus triumphed we would tread;
To all with willing hands dispense
The gifts of our benevolence.
JAMES MONTGOMERY. *Alt. and Abr.*

20

1
Father, my all in all Thou art,
My rest in toil, my ease in pain;
The healing of my broken heart;
In strife, my peace; in loss, my gain;

2
My smile beneath the cold world's frown;
In shame, my glory and my crown;
In want, my plentiful supply;
In weakness, my almighty power;

3
In bonds, my perfect liberty;
My light in evil's darkest hour;
In grief, my joy unspeakable;
My life in death, my all in all.

SECOND TUNE. L. M.

Ancient German.

THIRD TUNE. L. M.

Wareham. L. M.

WILLIAM KNAPP.

21

1
When God is seen with men to dwell,
And all creation makes anew,
What tongue can half the wonders tell?
What eye the dazzling glories view?

2
Celestial streams shall gently flow;
The wilderness shall joyful be;
Lilies on parchèd ground shall grow;
And gladness spring on every tree;

3
The weak be strong, the fearful bold,
The deaf shall hear, the dumb shall sing,
The lame shall walk, the blind behold,
And joy through all the earth shall ring.
H. BALLOU. *Alt. and Abr.*

22

1
The hopes Thy holy word supplies,
Its truth divine and precepts wise,
In each a heavenly beam I see,
And every beam conducts to Thee.

2
Almighty Lord, the sun shall fail,
The moon forget her nightly tale,
And deepest silence hush on high
The radiant chorus of the sky;—

3
But fixed for everlasting years,
Unmoved, amid the wreck of spheres,
Thy word shall shine in cloudless day,
When heaven and earth have passed away.
GRANT.

SECOND TUNE. L. M.

Old Melody.

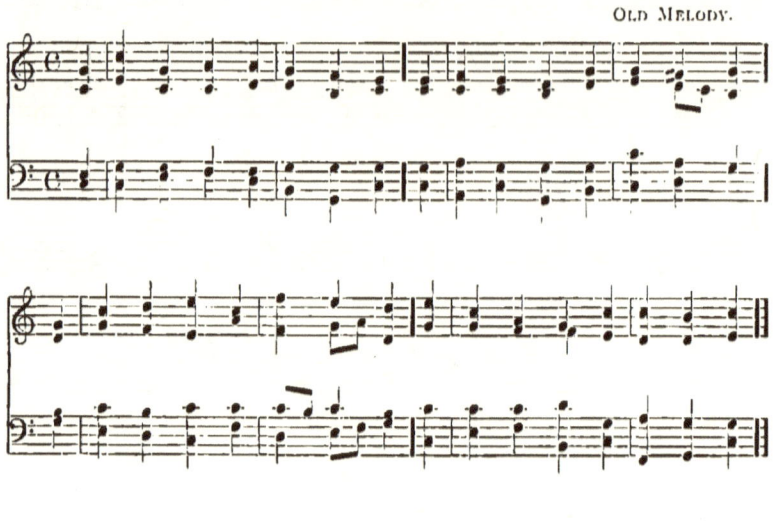

THIRD TUNE. L. M.

Federal Street. L. M.

H. K. Oliver.

23

1
How beauteous were the works divine,
That in thy meekness used to shine,
That lit thy lonely pathway, trod
In wondrous love, O Son of God!

2
Oh! who like thee so calm, so bright,
So pure, so made to live in light?
Oh! who like thee did ever go
So patient through a world of woe?

3
Oh! who like thee so humbly bore
The scorn, the scoffs of men, before?
So meek, forgiving, God-like, high,
So glorious in humility?

4
Oh, in thy light be mine to go,
Illuming all my way of woe!
And give me ever on the road
To trace thy footsteps, Son of God!

A. C. Coxe. *Alt.*

24

1
Thy will, almighty Father, Thine,
And Thine alone be ever done;
For Thou art Life and Truth and Love,
The great, eternal, holy One.

2
Reflectors, we, of all Thou art,
Of all the sunshine of Thy love,
No life from Thee we know apart,
But peace on earth of heaven above.

II.

SECOND TUNE. L. M.

S. S. Wesley.

THIRD TUNE. L. M.

ritard. ad lib.

Hursley. L. M.

FRANCIS JOSEPH HAYDN.
Arr. by WILLIAM HENRY MONK.

25

1
O Lord! where 'er Thy people meet,
There they behold Thy mercy-seat;
Where 'er they seek Thee, Thou art found,
And every place is hallowed ground.

2
For Thou, within no walls confined,
Inhabitest the humble mind;
Such ever bring Thee where they come,
And going, take Thee to their home.

3
Here we may prove the power of prayer
To strengthen faith and sweeten care;
To teach our faint desires to rise,
And bring all heaven before our eyes.

COWPER. *Alt.*

26

1
O God, whose presence glows in all,
Within, around us, and above!
Thy word we bless, Thy name we call,
Whose word is Truth, whose name is Love.

2
That love its holy influence pour
To keep us meek, and make us free;
And throw its binding blessing more
Round each with all, and all with Thee.

3
Send down its angel to our side,
Send in its calm upon the breast;
For we would know no other guide;
And we can need no other rest.

FROTHINGHAM. *Abr.*

SECOND TUNE. L. M.
Schumann.

THIRD TUNE. L. M.

Dulce Street. L. M.

J. Hatton.

27

"Take up thy cross," the Saviour said,
 If thou wouldst my disciple be;
Deny thyself, the world forsake,
 And humbly follow after me.

2
Take up thy cross, nor heed the shame;
 Nor let thy foolish pride rebel;
Thy Lord for thee the cross endured,
 He conquered sin, and death, and hell.

3
Take up thy cross, then, in His strength,
 And calmly every danger brave;
'T will guide thee to a better home,
 And lead to victory o'er the grave.

28

God is the Life, the Truth, the Way
Which leads unto the perfect day,
The Way which mortals should adore,
If they would reach the unseen shore.

2
Come to this fount which flows for all,
Come, and accept the gracious call,
Jesus, who came the Way to show,
Has said, that all, the Way may know.

3
Press forward to the Horeb height,
Look up and thou shalt see the Light,
Acquaint thyself at once with Love,
And Truth shall guide to Light above.
                              Mrs. Keyes.

SECOND TUNE. L. M.

Berthold Tours.

THIRD TUNE. L. M.

CHRISTIAN SCIENCE HYMNAL.

Hamburg. L. M.

Arr. by LOWELL MASON.

29

1
When Jesus, our great Master, came
To teach us in his Father's name,
In every act, in every thought,
He lived the precepts which he taught.

2
So let our lips and lives express
The holy gospel we profess;
So let our works and virtues shine,
To prove the doctrine all divine.

3
Thus shall we best proclaim abroad,
The honors of our Saviour, God,
When the salvation reigns within,
And grace subdues the claim of sin.

30

1
If my immortal Saviour lives,
Then my immortal life is sure;
His word a firm foundation gives;
Here may I build, and rest secure.

2
Here let my faith unshaken dwell;
Forever sure the promise stands;
Not all the claims of earth or hell
Can e'er dissolve the sacred bands.

3
Here, O my heart, thy trust repose;
If Jesus is forever mine,
Not death itself — that last of foes —
Shall break a union so divine.

SECOND TUNE. L. M.

OLD MELODY.

THIRD TUNE. L. M.

Hebron. L. M.

LOWELL MASON.

31

1
The Christain warrior, see him stand
 In the whole armor of his God;
The Spirit's sword is in his hand;
 His feet are with the gospel shod.

2
In panoply of truth complete,
 Salvation's helmet on his head,
With righteousness, a breastplate meet,
 And faith's broad shield before him spread.

3
With this omnipotence he moves;
 From this the alien armies flee;
Till more than conqueror he proves,
 Through Christ, who gives him victory.

4
Thus strong in his Redeemer's strength,
 Sin, death and hell he tramples down,—
Fights the good fight; and takes at length,
 Through mercy, an immortal crown.

32

1
I cannot always trace the way
 Where Thou, Almighty One, dost move;
But I can always, always say,
 That God is love, that God is love.

2
Yes, God is love;—a thought like this,
 Can every gloomy thought remove,
And turn all tears, all woes, to bliss,
 For God is love, for God is love.

SECOND TUNE. L. M.

BARNBY.

THIRD TUNE. L. M.

ritard. ad lib.

Ward. L. M.

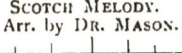

33

1

How sweetly flowed the gospel sound
From lips of gentleness and grace,
When listening thousands gather'd round,
And joy and reverence filled the place!

2

From heaven he came, of heaven he spoke,
To heaven he led his followers way;
Dark clouds of gloomy night he broke,
Unveiling an immortal day.

3

"Come, wanderers, to my Father's home;
Come, all ye weary ones, and rest:"

Yes, sacred Teacher, we will come,
Obey thee, love thee, and be blest.

JOHN BOWRING.

34

1

O Love Divine, whose constant beam
Shines on the eyes that will not see,
And waits to bless us while we dream,
Thou leav'st us when we turn from Thee!

2

Nor bounds, nor clime, nor creed Thou know'st:
Wide as our need, Thy favors fall;
The white wings of the Holy Ghost
Stoop, unseen, o'er the heads of all.

JOHN G. WHITTIER. *Abr.*

SECOND TUNE.

Edward Miller, Mus. Doc.

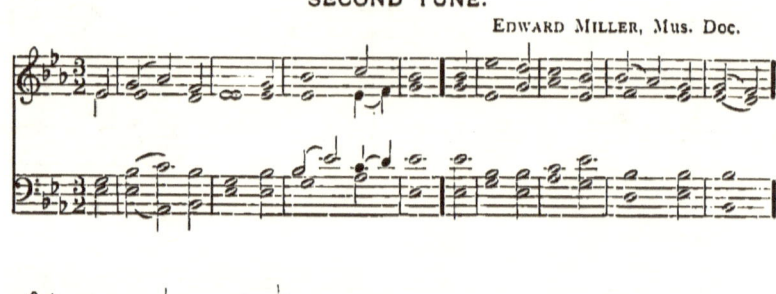

THIRD TUNE. L. M.

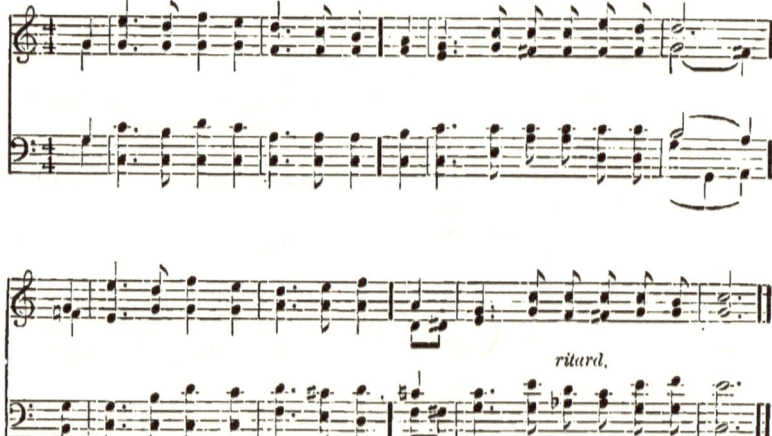

ritard.

Rockingham. L. M.

LOWELL MASON.

35

1
One cup of healing oil and wine,
One offering laid on mercy's shrine,
Is thrice more grateful, Lord, to Thee,
Than lifted eye or bended knee.

2
In true and inward faith we trace
The source of every outward grace;
Within the pious heart it plays,
A living fount of joy and praise.

3
Kind deeds of peace and love betray
Where'er the stream has found its way;
But, where these spring not rich and fair,
The stream has never wandered there.

W. H. DRUMMOND.

36

1
The lifted eye, and bended knee,
Are but vain homage, Lord, to Thee;
In vain our lips Thy praise prolong,
The heart, a stranger to the song.

2
The pure, the humble, contrite mind,
Sincere, and to Thy will resigned,
To Thee a nobler offering yields,
Than Sheba's groves, or Sharon's fields.

3
Love God and man — this great command,
Doth on eternal pillars stand;
This did Thine ancient prophets teach,
And this Thy Well-Belovèd preach.

SECOND TUNE. L. M.

G. M. Garrett.

THIRD TUNE. L. M.

The small notes are for accompaniment only.

Linwood. L. M.

GIOACCHIMO ROSSINI.

37

1
Be true and list the voice within,
　Be true unto thy high ideal,
Thy perfect self, that knows no sin—
　That self that is the only real.

2
God is the only perfect One:
　My perfect self, one must it be
With God, then,—and that thought begun
　It solveth all the mystery.

3
If true to God, and God is Love,
　Then true to Love deduce we then;
"Be true" means, true to God above,
　To self, and to our fellow-men.

38

1
High in the heavens, eternal God!
　Thy goodness in full glory shines;
Thy truth shall break through every cloud
　That vails and darkens Thy designs.

2
For ever firm Thy justice stands,
　As mountains their foundations keep:
Wise are the wonders of Thy hands;
　Thy judgments are a mighty deep.

3
Life, like a fountain rich and free,
　Springs from the presence of my Lord;
And in Thy light we all shall see
　The glories promised in Thy word.

　　　　　　　I. WATTS. *Alt. and Abr.*

SECOND TUNE. L. M.

E. HODGES, Mus. Doc.

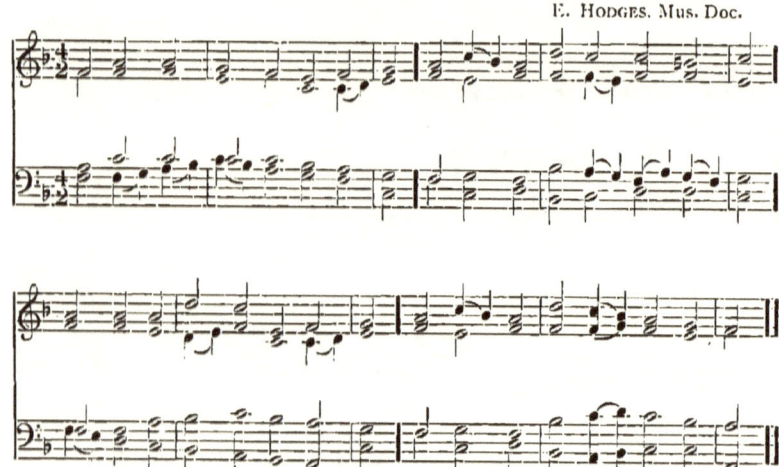

THIRD TUNE. L. M.

*Bera. L. M. 6l.

J. E. Gould.

39

1

He that has God his guardian made,
Shall under the Almighty's shade
 Secure and undisturbed abide;
Thus to myself of Him I'll say,
He is my fortress and my stay,
 My God, in whom I will confide.

2

His tender love and watchful care
Shall free thee from the fowler's snare
 And from the noisome pestilence;
He over thee His wings shall spread,
And cover thy unguarded head;
 His truth shall be thy strong defence.

3

Because with well-placed confidence
Thou mak'st the Lord thy sure defence,
 Thy refuge, even God most high;
Therefore no ill on thee shall come,
Nor to thy heaven-protected home
 Shall overwhelming plagues draw nigh.

*40

1

Press on, dear traveller, press on!
I am the Way, the Truth, the Life,
It is the strait and narrow way
That leads to that eternal day,
That turns the darkness into light,
That buries wrong and honors right.

2

Press on! and know that God is all.
He is the Life, the Truth, the Love.
It is the way the Saviour trod,
It is the way that leads to God,
Think of the word, "No cross, no crown;"
Though tasks are sore, be not cast down.

Mrs. J. H. Bell.

*When singing Hymn 40 repeat first half of the tune instead of first and third lines.

CHRISTIAN SCIENCE HYMNAL. 41

*SECOND TUNE. L. M. 6l.

WILLIAM HENRY MONK, Mus. Doc.

*THIRD TUNE. L. M. 6l.

The small notes are for accompaniment only.
*When used for Hymn 40 repeat first half of the tune instead of first and third lines.

Ortonville. C. M.

THOMAS HASTINGS.

41

1
"I am the way, the truth, the life,"
  Our blessed Master said;
And whoso to the Father comes,
  ||: Must in my pathway tread. :||

2
A way, it is not hedged with forms,
  A truth, too large for creeds,
A life, indwelling, deep and broad,
  ||: That meets the heart's great needs. :||

3
To point that living way, to speak
  That truth "which makes men free,"
To bring that quickening life from heaven,
  ||: Is highest ministry. :||

42

1
The Spirit breathes upon the word,
  And brings the truth to sight;
Precepts and promises afford
  A sanctifying light.

2
The hand that gave it, still supplies
  The gracious light and heat;
Its truths upon the nations rise,—
  They rise, but never set.

3
Let everlasting thanks be thine,
  For such a bright display,
As makes a world of darkness shine
  With beams of heavenly day.

W. COWPER. *Abr.*

SECOND TUNE. C. M.

(Sir H. W. Baker.) W. H. Monk.

THIRD TUNE. C. M.

Dedham. C. M.
Wm. Gardiner.

43

1
Faith grasps the blessing she desires,
  Hope points the upward gaze;
And Love, celestial Love, inspires
  The eloquence of praise.

2
But sweeter far the still small voice,
  Unheard by human ear,
When God has made the heart rejoice,
  And dried the bitter tear.

3
No accents flow, no words ascend;
  All utterance faileth there;
But God Himself doth comprehend
  And answer silent prayer.

44

1
Happy the heart where graces reign,
  Where love inspires the breast:
Love is the brightest of the train,
  And strengthens all the rest.

2
Knowledge — alas! 'tis all in vain,
  And all in vain our fear;
Our stubborn sins will fight and reign,
  If love be absent there.

3
This is the grace that lives and sings,
  When faith and hope shall cease;
'Tis this shall strike our joyful strings,
  In brightest realms of bliss.

SECOND TUNE. C. M.

James Comley.

THIRD TUNE. C. M.

Coronation. C. M.

OLIVER HOLDEN.

45

1
God's glory is a wondrous thing,
　Most strange in all its ways,
‖: And of all things on earth, least like
　What men agree to praise. :‖

2
Oh, blest is he to whom is given
　The instinct that can tell
‖: That God is on the field, when He
　Is most invisible! :‖

3
And blest is he who can divine
　Where right doth really lie,
‖: And dares to take the side that seems
　Wrong to man's blindfold eye! :‖

4
And right is right, since God is God;
　And right the day must win;
‖: To doubt would be disloyalty,
　To falter would be sin! :‖

F. W. FABER. *Alt.*

46

1
We say to all men far and near
　That Christ has risen again;
‖: That He is with us now and here,
　And ever shall remain. :‖

2
He lives; His presence hath not ceased,
　Though foes and fears be rife;
‖: And thus we hail the gospel feast,
　A world renewed to life! :‖

NOVALIS. *Abr.*

SECOND TUNE. C. M.

Vincent Novello.

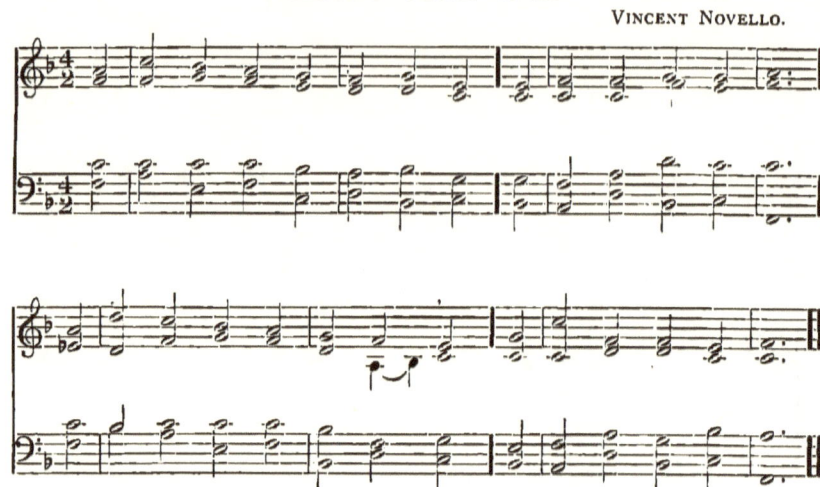

THIRD TUNE. C. M.

Oaksville. C. M.

C. ZEUNER.

47

1

Man is the noblest work of God,
 His beauty, power, and grace,
Immortal; perfect as His Mind
 Reflected, face to face.

2

God could not make imperfect man
 His model Infinite;
Unhallowed thought He could not plan—
 Love's work and Love must fit.

3

Life, Truth, and Love the pattern make,
 Christ is the perfect heir;
The clouds of sense roll back, and show
 The form divinely fair.

4

And man does stand as God's own child,
 The image of His Love.

Let gladness ring from every tongue,
 And Heaven and earth approve.

ALICE DAYTON.

48

1

Scorn not the slightest word or deed,
 Nor deem it void of power;
There's fruit in each wind-wafted seed,
 Waiting its natal hour.

2

No act falls fruitless; none can tell
 How vast its power may be;
Nor what results enfolded dwell
 Within it silently.

3

Work and despair not; bring thy mite,
 Nor care how small it be;
God is with all that serve the right
 The holy, true, and free.

SECOND TUNE. L. M.

Edward J. Hopkins, Mus. Doc.

THIRD TUNE. C. M.

The small notes are for accompaniment only.

CHRISTIAN SCIENCE HYMNAL.

Arlington. C. M.

THOMAS A. ARNE.

49

1
We may not climb the heavenly steeps
To bring the Lord Christ down;
In vain we search the lowest deeps,
For Him no depths can drown.

2
But warm, sweet, tender, even yet
A present help is He;
And faith has yet its Olivet,
And love its Galilee.

3
The healing of the seamless dress
Is by our beds of pain;
We touch Him in life's throng and press,
And we are whole again.

4
O Lord and Master of us all,
Whate'er our name or sign,
We own Thy sway, we hear Thy call,
We test our lives by Thine!

J. G. WHITTIER. *Abr.*

50

1
Whatever dims thy sense of truth,
Or stains thy purity,
Though light as breath of summer air,
Count it as sin to thee.

2
Preserve the tablet of thy thoughts
From every blemish free,
While the Redeemer's lowly faith
Its temple makes with thee.

3
And pray of God, that grace be given
To tread this narrow way:—
How dark soever it may seem,
It leads to cloudless day.

SECOND TUNE. C. M.

H. J. GAUNTLETT, Mus. Doc.

THIRD TUNE. C. M.

Manoah. C. M.

Arr. from G. Rossini.

51

1
How bless'd are they whose hearts are pure,
From guile their thoughts are free;
To them shall God reveal Himself,
They shall His glory see.

2
They truly rest upon His word,
In fullest light of love,
In this their trust, they ask no more
Than guidance from above.

3
They who in faith unmix'd with doubt
Th'engrafted word receive,
Whom the first sign of heavenly power
Persuades, and they believe;

4
For them far greater things than these
Doth Christ the Lord prepare;
Whose bliss no heart of man can reach
No human voice declare.

52

1
Oh! ever on our earthly path
Some gleam of glory lies;
And heav'n is all around us now,
If we but lift our eyes.

2
Lift up the heart, lift up the mind!
Until the grace be given,
That, while we travail yet on earth,
Our hearts may be in heaven.

SECOND TUNE. C. M.

A. R. REINAGLE.

THIRD TUNE. C. M.

Naomi. C. M.

H. G. NAEGELI.
Arr. by LOWELL MASON.

53

1
Help us to help each other, Lord,
  Each other's cross to bear;
Let each his friendly aid afford,
  And feel his brother's care.

2
Help us to build each other up,
  Our little stock improve;
Increase our faith, confirm our hope,
  And perfect us in Love.

3
Up into Thee, our living Head,
  Let us in all things grow;

Till Thou hast made us free indeed,
  And spotless here below.

54

1
Church of the ever-living God,
  The Father's gracious choice,
Amid the voices of this earth
  How mighty is Thy voice!

2
Not many rich or noble called,
  Not many great or wise;
They whom God makes His kings and priests
  Are poor in human eyes.

H. BONAR. *Alt. and Abr.*

SECOND TUNE. C. M.

John Hopkins.

THIRD TUNE. C. M.

Maitland. C. M.

G. N. Allen.

55

1
How lovely are Thy dwellings, Lord,
From noise and trouble free;
How beautiful the sweet accord
Of those who pray to Thee!

2
Lord God of Hosts, that reign'st on high,
They are the truly blest
Who on Thee only will rely,
In Thee alone will rest.

3
For God the Lord, both sun and shield,
Gives grace and glory bright;
No good from him shall be withheld
Whose ways are just and right.
Milton. *Alt. and Abr.*

56

1
Oh, speed thee, Christian, on thy way,
And to thy armor cling;
With girded loins the call obey,
That grace and mercy bring!

2
There is a battle to be fought,
An upward race to run;
A crown of glory to be sought,
A victory to be won.

3
Oh, faint not, Christian! not with sighs
Come thou before His throne:
The race must come before the prize,
The cross before the crown.
Anon.

SECOND TUNE. C. M.

Sir John Stainer, A. M., Mus. Doc.

THIRD TUNE. C. M.

Balerma. C. M.

HUGH WILSON.

57

1
How sweet, how heavenly is the sight,
 When those who love the Lord
In one another's peace delight,
 And so fulfil His word!

2
When, free from envy, scorn, and pride,
 Our wishes all above,
Each can his brother's failings hide,
 And show a brother's love!

3
Let love, in one delightful stream,
 Through every bosom flow;
And union sweet, and dear esteem
 In every action glow.

4
Love is the golden chain that binds
 The happy hearts above;
And he's an heir of heaven who finds
 His bosom glow with love.

J. SWAIN.

58

1
Beneath the thick but struggling cloud,
 We talk of Christain life;
The words of Jesus on our lips,
 Our hearts with man at strife.

2
Traditions, forms, and selfish aims
 Have dimmed the inner light;
Have closely veiled the spirit-world
 And angels from our sight.

3
Strong hearts and willing hands we need,
 Our temple to repair;
Remove the gathering dust of years,
 And show the model fair.

ANON.

CHRISTIAN SCIENCE HYMNAL. 59

SECOND TUNE. C. M.
JOHN RICHARDSON.

THIRD TUNE. C. M.

SOPRANO OR TENOR SOLO.

The small notes are for accompaniment only.

Evan. C. M.
Wm. H. Havergal.

59

1
Now to our loving Father, God,
A gladsome song begin;
His smile is on the world abroad,
His joy our hearts within.

2
We need not, Lord, our gladness leave,
To worship Thee aright;
Our joyfulness for praise receive!
Thou mak'st our lives so bright!

3
The pure in heart are always glad;
The smile of God they feel;
He doth the secret of His joy
To blameless hearts reveal.

Hymns and Tunes. Abr.

60

1
Speak gently, it is better far
To rule by love than fear;
Speak gently: let no harsh word mar
The good we may do here.

2
Speak gently to the erring: know
They must have toiled in vain;
Perchance unkindness made them so;
O win them back again.

3
Speak gently: 'tis a little thing,
Dropped in the heart's deep well;
The good, the joy that it may bring,
Eternity shall tell.

SECOND TUNE. C. M.

J. V. Roberts, Mus. Doc.

THIRD TUNE. C. M.

CHRISTIAN SCIENCE HYMNAL.

Azmon. C. M.

GLAZER. Arr. by DR. MASON.

61

1
Supreme in wisdom as in power,
   The Rock of Ages stands:
Canst thou not search His mind, and trace
   The working of His hands?

2
He gives the conquest to the weak,
   Supports the fainting heart;
And courage in the evil hour
   His heavenly aids impart.

3
Mere human energy shall faint,
   And youthful vigor cease;
But those who wait upon the Lord,
   In strength shall still increase.

4
They, with unwearied step, shall tread
   The path of life divine;

With growing ardor onward move,
   With growing brightness shine.
      WILLIAM CAMERON. *Alt. and Abr.*

62

1
Ye timid saints, fresh courage take!
   The clouds ye so much dread,
Are big with mercy, and will break
   In blessings on your head.

2
His purposes will ripen fast,
   Unfolding every hour;
The bud may have a bitter taste,
   But sweet will be the flower.

3
Blind unbelief is sure to err,
   And scan His work in vain;
God is His own interpreter,
   And He will make it plain.
      COWPER. *Alt. and Abr.*

SECOND TUNE. C. M.

Myles B. Foster.

THIRD TUNE. C. M.

Peterborough. C. M.   Ralph Harrison.

63

1
Walk in the light! so thou shalt know
That fellowship of love,
His Spirit only can bestow,
Who reigns in light above.

2
Walk in the light! and thou shalt find
Thy heart made truly His,
Who dwells in cloudless light enshrined
In whom no darkness is.

3
Walk in the light! and thou shalt own
Thy darkness passed away,
Because that Light hath on thee shone
In which is perfect day.

4
Walk in the light! and thou shalt see
Thy path, though thorny, bright,
For God by grace shall dwell with thee,
And God himself is Light.

          Bernard Barton. *Alt. and Abr.*

64

1
Joy to the world,—the Lord is come;
Let earth receive her King;
Let every heart prepare Him room,
And heaven and nature sing.

2
No more let sin and sorrow grow,
Nor thorns infest the ground,
He comes to make His blessings flow,
Far as the curse is found.

3
He rules the world with truth and grace,
And makes the nations prove
The glories of His righteousness,
And wonders of His love.

          I. Watts. *Abr.*

SECOND TUNE. C. M.

Thomas Wright.

THIRD TUNE. C. M.

Duet.

 **St. Agnes.** C. M.

J. B. DYKES.

65

1
City of God, how broad and far
  Outspread Thy walls sublime!
The true Thy chartered freemen are,
  Of every age and clime.

2
One holy Church, one army strong,
  One steadfast high intent,
One working band, one harvest-song,
  One King Omnipotent!

3
How gleam Thy watch-fires through the night,
  With never-fainting ray!
How rise Thy towers, serene and bright,
  To meet the dawning day!

4
In vain the surge's angry shock,
  In vain the drifting sands;
Unharmed, upon th' Eternal Rock,
  Th' Eternal City stands.

SAMUEL JOHNSON. *Abr.*

66

1
Planted in Christ, the living vine,
  This day, with one accord,
Ourselves, with humble faith and joy,
  We yield to Thee, O Lord!

2
Joined in one body may we be:
  One inward life partake;
One be our heart, one heavenly hope
  In every bosom wake.

S. F. SMITH. *Abr.*

Belmont. C. M.

JOHANN C. W. A. MOZART.

67

1
O for a faith that will not shrink,
  Though pressed by ev'ry foe;
That will not tremble on the brink
  Of any earthly woe;

2
A faith that shines more bright and clear
  When tempests rage without;
That when in danger knows no fear,
  In darkness feels no doubt;

3
Oh, give us such a faith as this,
  And then, whate'er may come,
We'll taste, e'en here the hallowed bliss
  Of an eternal home.

W. H. BATHURST. *Abr.*

68

1
I worship Thee, sweet Will of God,
  And all Thy ways adore;
And every day I live, I seem
  To love Thee more and more.

2
When obstacles and trials seem
  Like prison walls to be,
I do the little I can do,
  And leave the rest to Thee.

3
He always wins who sides with God,
  To him no chance is lost;
God's will is sweetest to him when
  It triumphs at his cost.

Rev. F. W. FABER. *Abr.*

Christmas. C. M.
G. F. Handel.

69

1
To us a Child of Hope is born,
 To us a Son is given;
Him shall the tribes of earth obey,
‖: Him all the hosts of heaven. :‖

2
His name shall be the Prince of Peace,
 For evermore adored;
The Wonderful, the Counsellor,
‖: The great and mighty Lord! :‖

3
His power, increasing, still shall spread;
 His reign no end shall know;
Justice shall guard His throne above,
‖: And peace abound below. :‖

John Morrison. *Abr.*

70

1
Lord! I have made Thy word my choice,
 My lasting heritage:
There shall my noblest powers rejoice,
‖: My warmest thoughts engage. :‖

2
I'll read the history of Thy love,
 And keep Thy law in sight,
While through the promises I rove,
‖: With ever-fresh delight. :‖

3
'T is a broad land of wealth unknown,
 Where springs of life arise;
Seeds of immortal bliss are sown,
‖: And hidden glory lies. :‖

I. Watts. *Alt. and Abr.*

SECOND TUNE. C. M.

Day's Psalter, 1563.

THIRD TUNE. C. M.

All Voices in Unison (or Solo.)

The small notes are for accompaniment only.

71

1

O Love! O Life! our faith and sight —
   Thy presence maketh one:
As, through transfigured clouds of white,
   We trace the noon-day sun.

2

We faintly hear, we dimly see,
   In differing phrase we pray;
But, dim or clear, we own in Thee
   The Light, the Truth, the Way.

3

To do Thy will is more than praise,
   As words are less than deeds;
And simple trust can find Thy ways
   We miss with chart of creeds.

4

Our Friend, our Brother, and our Lord,
   What may Thy service be?
Nor name, nor form, nor ritual word,
   But simply following Thee.

JOHN G. WHITTIER. *Abr.*

72

1

We walk by faith of joys to come;
   Faith lives upon His word;
But while the body is our home,
   We're absent from the Lord.

2

'Tis pleasant to believe Thy grace,
   But we had rather see;
We would be absent from the flesh,
   And present, Lord, with Thee.

I. WATTS. *Abr.*

SECOND TUNE. C. M.

E. H. Turpin.

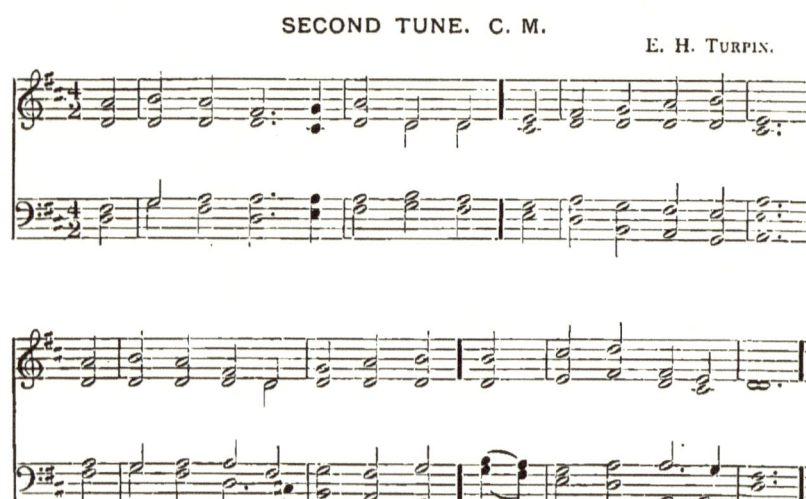

THIRD TUNE. C. M.

The small notes are to be sung, but much softer than the large ones.

Avon. C. M.

HUGH WILSON.

73

1
Our God is love; and all His saints
  His image bear below;
The heart with love to God inspired,
  With love to man will glow.

2
Teach us to love each other, Lord,
  As we are loved by Thee;
None who are truly born of God,
  Can live in enmity.

3
Heirs of the same immortal bliss,
  Our hopes and aims the same,
With bonds of love our hearts unite,
  With mutual love inflame.

4
So may the unbelieving world
  See how true Christians love;
And glorify our Saviour's grace,
  And seek that grace to prove.

74

1
Come, ye that know and fear the Lord,
  And raise your thoughts above:
Let every heart and voice accord,
  To sing that "God is love."

2
This precious truth His word declares,
  And all His mercies prove;
Jesus, the gift of gifts, appears,
  To show that "God is love."

G. BURDER. *Abr.*

SECOND TUNE. C. M.

Sangster.

THIRD TUNE. C. M.

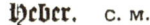

75

1
Thou art the Way: to Thee alone
From sin and death we flee;
And he who would the Father seek,
Must seek Him, Lord, by Thee.

2
Thou art the Truth: Thy word alone
True wisdom can impart;
Thou only canst unfold that Truth,
And purify the heart.

3
Thou art the Life: the rending tomb
Proclaims Thy conquering arm;
And those who put their trust in Thee
Nor death nor hell shall harm.

4
Thou art the Way, the Truth, the Life,
Grant us that Way to know;
That Truth to keep, that Life to win,
Whose joys eternal flow.

GEORGE W. DOANE. *Alt.*

76

1
Walk with your God, along the road
Your strength He will renew;
Wait on the everlasting God,
And He will work with you.

2
Ye shall not faint, ye shall not fail,
Made in the spirit strong;
Each task divine ye still shall hail,
And blend it with a song.

T. H. GILL.

SECOND TUNE. C. M.

Henry Lahee.

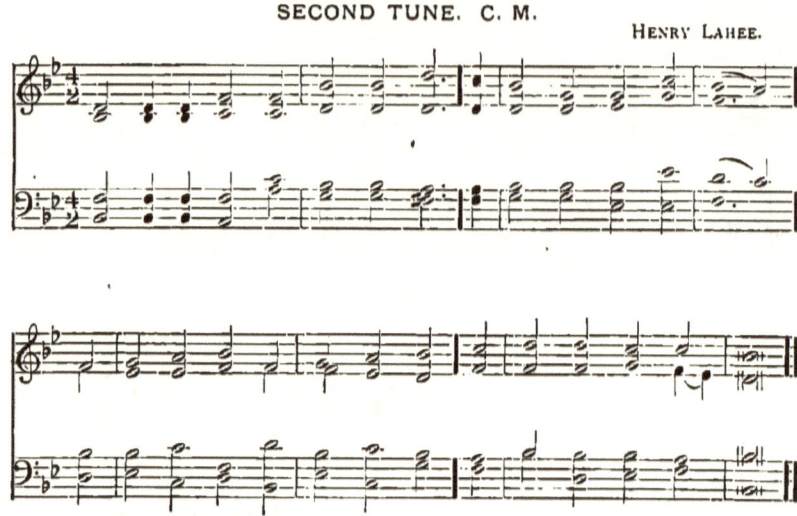

THIRD TUNE. C. M.

 **Colchester.** C. M.

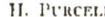 H. PURCELL.

77

1

Immortal Love, for ever full,
 For ever flowing free,
For ever shared, for ever whole,
 A never-ebbing sea!

2

Our outward lips confess the name
 All other names above;
But love alone knows whence it came,
 And comprehendeth love.

3

Blow, winds of God, awake and blow
 The mists of earth away!
Shine out, O Light divine, and show
 How wide and far we stray!

4

The letter fails, the systems fall,
 And every symbol wanes:
The Spirit over-brooding all,
 Eternal Love, remains.

JOHN G. WHITTIER.

78

1

I cannot walk in darkness long,
 My Light is by my side;
I cannot stumble or go wrong
 While following such a guide.

2

He is my stay and my defence,
 How shall I fail or fall?
My keeper is Omnipotence;
 My Ruler ruleth all.

CAROLINE A. MASON. *Abr.*

SECOND TUNE. C. M.

Rev. F. A. J. Hervey.

THIRD TUNE. C. M.

Solo for Soprano or Tenor.

Solo for Alto. (*Sing one octave lower than written.*)

Coventry. C. M.

ENGLISH MELODY.

79

1
The God who made both heaven and earth,
  And all that they contain,
Will never quit His steadfast truth
  Nor make His promise vain.

2
The poor, oppressed by all their wrong,
  Are saved by His decree;
He gives the hungry needful food,
  And sets the pris'ners free.

3
By Him the blind receive their sight,
  The weak and fall'n He rears;
With kind regard and tender love
  He for the righteous cares.

80

1
Bright was the guiding star that led,
  With mild, benignant ray,
The Gentiles to the lowly shed
  Where the Redeemer lay.

2
But, lo! a brighter, clearer light,
  Now points to His abode:
It shines through sin and sorrow's night,
  To guide us to our Lord.

3
Oh, haste to follow where it leads!
  The gracious call obey,
Be rugged wilds or flowery meads
  The Christian's destined way.

HARRIET AUBER. *Abr.*

SECOND TUNE. C. M.

Isaac Smith.

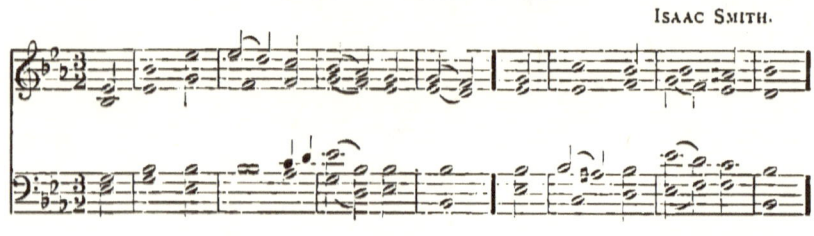

THIRD TUNE. C. M.

Southport. C. M.

GEORGE KINGSLEY.

81

1
In atmosphere of love divine,
  We live, and move, and breathe;
Though mortal eyes may see it not;
  'T is sense that would deceive.

2
The Principle of being, God,
  Is with us ev'rywhere;
He holds us perfect in His love,
  And we His image bear.

3
The mortal sense we must destroy,
  If we would bring to light
The wonders of eternal Mind,
  Where sense is lost in sight.

82

1
The loving friend to all who bowed
  Beneath life's weary load,
From lips baptized in humble prayer,
  His consolations flowed.

2
The faithful witness to the truth,
  His just rebuke was hurled
Out from a heart that burned to break
  The fetters of the world.

3
No hollow rite, no lifeless creed,
  His piercing glance could bear;
But longing hearts which sought Him found
  That God and heaven were there.

SAMUEL LONGFELLOW.

SECOND TUNE. C. M.

Mr. Denby in "Barber's Psalm Tunes." 1687.

THIRD TUNE. C. M.

Dundee. C. M.

GUILLAUME FRANC.

83

1
O pure Reformers! not in vain
　Your trust in human kind;
The good which bloodshed could not gain,
　Your peaceful zeal shall find.

2
The truths ye urge are borne abroad
　By every wind and tide;
The voice of nature and of God
　Speaks out upon your side.

3
Press on! and, if we may not share
　The glory of your fight,
We'll ask at least, in earnest prayer,
　God's blessing on the Right.

JOHN G. WHITTIER.

84

1
Beneath the shadow of the cross,
　As earthly hopes remove,
His new commandment Jesus gives,—
　His blessed word of love.

2
O bond of union, strong and deep!
　O bond of perfect peace!
Not e'en the lifted cross can harm,
　If we but hold to this.

3
Then, Jesus, be thy Spirit ours;
　And swift our feet shall move
To deeds of pure self-sacrifice,
　And the sweet tasks of love.

SAMUEL LONGFELLOW.

SECOND TUNE. C. M.

H. S. Irons.

THIRD TUNE. C. M.

St. Martin's. C. M.   Wm. Tansur.

85

1
One holy Church of God appears
  Through every age and race,
Unwasted by the lapse of years,
  Unchanged by changing place.

2
From oldest time, on farthest shores,
  Beneath the pine or palm,
One Unseen Presence she adores,
  With silence or with psalm.

3
Her priests are all God's faithful sons,
  To serve the world raised up;
The pure in heart her baptized ones;
  Love, her communion-cup.

Samuel Longfellow. Abr.

86

1
Make channels for the streams of love,
  Where they may broadly run;
And love has overflowing streams,
  To fill them every one.

2
But if at any time we cease
  Such channels to provide,
The very founts of love for us
  Will soon be parched and dried.

3
For we must share, if we would keep
  That blessing from above:
Ceasing to give, we cease to have,
  Such is the law of love.

Richard C. Trench.

SECOND TUNE. C. M.

WILLIAM STEVENSON HOYTE.

THIRD TUNE. C. M.

Eckhardtsheim. C. M.

C. Zeuner.

87

1
Lowly in heart to all who sought,
  A friend and servant found;
He washed their feet, he wiped their tears,
  And healed each bleeding wound.

2
Midst keen reproach and cruel scorn,
  Patient and meek he stood;
His foes, ungrateful, sought his life;
  He labored for their good.

3
Jesus our pattern and our guide
  His cross may we all bear,
O may we tread his holy steps,
  His joy and glory share.

88

1
Prayer is the heart's sincere desire,
  Uttered or unexpressed;
The motion of a hidden fire
  That trembles in the breast.

2
Prayer is the simplest form of speech
  That infant lips can try;
Prayer the sublimest strains that reach
  The Majesty on high.

3
Prayer is the Christian's vital breath,
  The Christian's native air:
His watchword overcometh death —
  He enters heaven with prayer.

J. Montgomery. *Alt. and Abr.*

CHRISTIAN SCIENCE HYMNAL.

SECOND TUNE. C. M.

Rev. J. B. Dykes, Mus. Doc.

THIRD TUNE. C. M.

St. Asaph.   C. M. D.

J. M. GIORNOVICHI.

89

1
It came upon the midnight clear,
  That glorious song of old,
The angels bending near the earth
  Their wondrous story told;
Peace on the earth, good-will to men,
  From heaven's all-gracious King;
The world in solemn stillness lay
  To hear the angels sing.

2
O ye, beneath life's crushing load,
  Whose forms are bending low,
Who toil along the climbing way
  With painful steps and slow!
Look now, for glad and golden hours
  Come swiftly on the wing;
O rest beside the weary road,
  And hear the angels sing.

3
For lo, the days are hastening on,
  By prophets seen of old,
When with the ever-circling years
  Shall come the time foretold,
When the new heaven and earth shall own
  The Prince of Peace their King,
And the whole world send back the song
  Which now the angels sing.

90

1
Oh! not alone with outward sign,
  Of fear, or voice from heaven,
The message of a truth divine,
  The call of God, is given;
Awakening in the human heart,
  Love for the true and right,
Zeal for the Christian's better part,
  Strength for the Christian's fight.

2
Though heralded by naught of fear,
  Or outward sign or show;
Though only to the inward ear
  It whispers soft and low;
Though dropping as the manna fell,
  Unseen, yet from above.
Holy and gentle heed it well,
  The call to Truth and Love.
                                WHITTIER.

CHRISTIAN SCIENCE HYMNAL. 91

SECOND TUNE. C. M. D.

ARTHUR SULLIVAN.

THIRD TUNE. C. M. D.

The small notes are for accompaniment only.

CHRISTIAN SCIENCE HYMNAL.

Brattle Street. C. M. D.

I. PLEYEL.

91

1
O Lord, I would delight in Thee,
  And on Thy care depend;
To Thee in every trouble flee,
  My best, my only Friend!
When all material streams are dried,
  Thy fullness is the same;
May I with this be satisfied,
  And glory in Thy name.

2
No good in creatures can be found,
  But may be found in Thee;
I must have all things, and abound,
  While God is God to me.
O that I had a stronger faith,
  To look within the veil,
To credit what my Saviour saith,
  Whose word can never fail.

3
He that has made my heaven secure,
  Will here all good provide;
While Christ is rich, can I be poor?
  What can I want beside?
O God, I cast my care on Thee;
  I triumph and adore;
Henceforth my great concern shall be
  To love and praise Thee more.

JOHN RYLAND.

92

1
Eternal Mind the Potter is,
  And thought, the eternal clay.
The hand that fashions is divine;
  His works pass not away.
Man is the noblest work of God.
  His beauty, power, and grace,
Immortal; perfect as His Mind
  Reflected, face to face.

2
God could not make imperfect man
  His model Infinite;
Unhallowed thought He could not plan—
  Love's work and Love must fit.
Life, Truth, and Love the pattern make,
  Christ is the perfect heir;
The clouds of sense roll back, and show
  The form divinely fair.

3
God's will is done; His kingdom come.
  The Potter's work is plain.
The longing to be good and true
  Has brought the Light again;
And Man does stand as God's own child,
  The image of His Love.
Let gladness ring from every tongue,
  And heaven and earth approve.

ALICE DAYTON.

The small notes are for accompaniment only.

Dennis. S. M.

Arr. by LOWELL MASON.

93

1
How gentle God's commands!
How kind His precepts are!
Come, cast your burdens on the Lord,
And trust His constant care.

2
Beneath His watchful eye
His saints securely dwell;
That hand which bears creation up
Shall guard His children well.

3
His goodness stands approved,
Unchanged from day to day:
I'll drop my burden at His feet,
And bear a song away.

P. DODDRIDGE. *Abr.*

94

1
Our heaven is everywhere,
If we but love our God,
Unswerving tread the narrow way,
And ever shun the broad.

2
'T is where the trusting heart
Bows meekly to its grief,
Still looking up with earnest faith
For comfort and relief.

3
Wherever truth abides,
Sweet peace is ever there;
If we but love and serve the Lord,
Our heaven is everywhere.

MISS FLETCHER. *Alt. and Abr.*

SECOND TUNE. S. M.

JOHN HOPKINS.

THIRD TUNE. S. M.

95

1
O Spirit, source of light,
  Thy grace is unconfined;
Dispel the gloomy shades of night,
  Reveal the light of Mind.

2
Now to our eyes display
  The truth Thy words reveal;
Cause us to run the heavenly way,
  Delighting in Thy will.

3
Thy teachings make us know
  The myst'ries of Thy love,
The vanity of things below,
  The joy of things above.
                    ANON.

96

1
Imposture shrinks from light,
  And dreads the piercing eye;
But sacred truths the test invite,
  They bid us search and try.

2
With understanding blest,
  Created to be free,
Our faith on man we dare not rest,
  Subject to none but Thee.

3
The truth Thou dost impart,
  May we with firmness own;
Abhorring each evasive art,
  And fearing Thee alone.
              SCOTT. *Alt. and Abr.*

SECOND TUNE. S. M.

Sir John Stainer, M. A, Mus. Doc.

THIRD TUNE. S. M.

State Street. S. M.

JONATHAN C. WOODMAN.

97
1
Come to the land of peace;
 From shadows come away;
Where all the sounds of weeping cease,
 And storms no more have sway.

2
Fear hath no dwelling here;
 But pure repose and love
Breathe through the bright, celestial air
 The spirit of the dove.

3
In this divine abode
 Change leaves no sadd'ning trace;
Come, trusting heart, come to thy God,
 Thy holy resting-place.

Alt. and Abr.

98
1
Let party names no more
 The Christian world o'erspread;
Gentile and Jew, and bond and free,
 Are one in Christ their head.

2
Among the saints on earth,
 Let mutual love be found;
Heirs of the same inheritance,
 With mutual blessings crowned.

3
Thus will the church below
 Resemble that above;
Where streams of pleasure ever flow,
 And every heart is love.

B. BEDDOME.

Used by permission of Oliver Ditson Company, owners of the copyright.

SECOND TUNE. S. M.

William Henry Monk, Mus. Doc.

THIRD TUNE. S. M.

Laban. S. M.

LOWELL MASON.

99

1
Thine is a living way;
 In death it has no part;
From fear of all disease and sin,
 It will relieve the heart.

2
Oh blessed, blessed Light!
 Oh joyful, joyful news!
Thy law is Life, Thy way is peace,
 No other can we choose.

3
The Spirit's sweet control
 Freely we will confess,—
Fly to Thine outstretched arms of love,
 And there find health and rest.

M. J. H. ZINK. *Abr.*

100

1
Teach me, my God and King,
 In all things Thee to see;
And what I do in any thing,
 To do it as for Thee.

2
To scorn the senses' sway
 While still to Thee I tend;
In all I do, be Thou the way,—
 In all be Thou the end.

3
If done beneath Thy laws,
 E'en servile labors shine;
Hallowed is toil, if this the cause,
 The meanest work divine.

Rev. GEORGE HERBERT. *Abr.*

SECOND TUNE. S. M.

JAMES WATSON.

THIRD TUNE. S. M.

The small notes are for accompaniment only.

St. Thomas. S. M.

WILLIAM TANSUR.

101

1
'T is God the Spirit leads
  In paths before unknown;
The work to be performed is ours,
  The strength is all His own.

2
Supported by His grace,
  We still pursue our way;
Assured that we shall reach the prize,
  Secure in endless day.

3
'T is He that works to will,
  'T is He that works to do;
His is the power by which we act,
  His be the glory too.

MONTGOMERY. *Alt.*

102

1
Servants of Christ, arise,
  And gird you for the toil.
The dew of promise from the skies
  Already cheers the soil.

2
Go where the sick recline,
  Where mourning hearts deplore;
And where the sons of sorrow pine,
  Dispense your hallowed lore.

3
So shall you share the wealth,
  That earth may ne'er despoil,
And the blest gospel's saving health
  Repay your arduous toil.

MRS. LYDIA H. SIGOURNEY. *Abr.*

SECOND TUNE. S. M.

H. J. Gauntlett, Mus. Doc.

THIRD TUNE. S. M.

The small notes are for accompaniment only.

Boylston. S. M.

LOWELL MASON.

103

1
Soldiers of Christ, arise,
 And put your armor on,
Strong is the strength which God supplies
 Through His eternal Son.

2
Stand then in His great might,
 With all His strength endued,
And take, to arm you for the fight,
 The panoply of God.

3
From strength to strength go on;
 Wrestle, and fight, and pray;
Tread all the powers of darkness down,
 And win the well-fought day.
C. WESLEY. *Abr.*

104

1
Heirs of unending life,
 While yet we sojourn here,
Oh, let us our salvation work
 With trembling and with fear.

2
God will support our hearts,
 With might before unknown;
The work to be performed is ours,
 The strength is all His own.

3
'T is He that works to will,
 'T is He that works to do;
His is the power by which we act,
 His be the glory too!
ANON.

SECOND TUNE. S. M.

Sir Herbert Oakeley, LL. D., Mus. Doc.

THIRD TUNE. S. M.

105

1

Ye servants of the Lord!
  Each in his office wait,
Observant of His heavenly word,
  And watchful at His gate.

2

Let all your lamps be bright,
  And trim the golden flame;
Gird up your loins as in His sight,
  For Perfect is His name.

3

Watch,— 'tis your Lord's command;
  And while we speak He's near;
Mark the first signal of His hand,
  And ready all appear.

4

Oh, happy servant he,
  In such a posture found!
He shall his Lord with rapture see,
  And be with honor crowned.

DODDRIDGE.

106

1

Ye messengers of Christ!
  His sovereign voice obey;
Arise, and follow where He leads,
  And peace attend your way.

2

The Master, whom you serve,
  Will needful strength bestow;
Depending on His promised aid,
  With sacred courage go.

3

Mountains shall sink to plains,
  And hell in vain oppose;
The cause is God's — and will prevail,
  In spite of all His foes

Mrs. VOKE.

CHRISTIAN SCIENCE HYMNAL.

SECOND TUNE. S. M.

Old German. KÖLNER GESANGBUCH.

THIRD TUNE. S. M.

The small notes are for accompaniment only.

Olmutz. S. M.

Arr. by Dr. Mason.

107

1
Oh do not bar your mind
  Against the light of Good;
But open wide, let in the Word,
  And Truth will be your food.

2
It will from error free
  Your long-enslaved mind;
And bring the light of liberty
  Where it shall be enshrined.

3
Hid treasures it reveals
  To all who know its power,
And all who will may light receive,
  In this most gracious hour.

4
Then open wide your heart
  To Truth and Light and Love;
You then shall know your Life is hid
  With Christ in God above.

CHARLES PARSONS. *Abr*

108

1
Sow in the morn thy seed,
  At eve hold not thy hand;
To doubt and fear give thou no heed;
  Broad-cast it o'er the land.

2
And duly shall appear
  In verdure, beauty, strength,
The tender blade, the stalk, the ear,
  And the full corn at length.

J. MONTGOMERY

SECOND TUNE. S. M.

Old German. MÜLLER'S CHORALBUCH. 1754.

THIRD TUNE. S. M.

Silver Street. S. M.

I. SMITH.

109

1
Happy the man, who knows
His Master to obey;
Whose life of care and labor flows,
Where God points out the way.

2
He riseth to his task,
Soon as the word is given;
Nor waits, nor doth a question ask,
When orders come from Heaven.

3
Nothing he calls his own;
Nothing he hath to say;
His feet are shod for God alone,
And God alone obey.

4
Give us, O God, this mind,
Which waits for Thy command,
And doth its highest pleasure find
In Thy great work to stand.

Rev. THOMAS COGSWELL UPHAM.

110

1
Make haste, O man, to do
Whatever must be done;
Thou hast no time to lose in sloth,
When all to Truth must come.

2
Up then, with speed and work;
Fling ease and self away—
This is no time for thee to sleep—
Up, watch, and work, and pray!

H. BONAR. *Alt. and Abr.*

SECOND TUNE. S. M.
Anon.

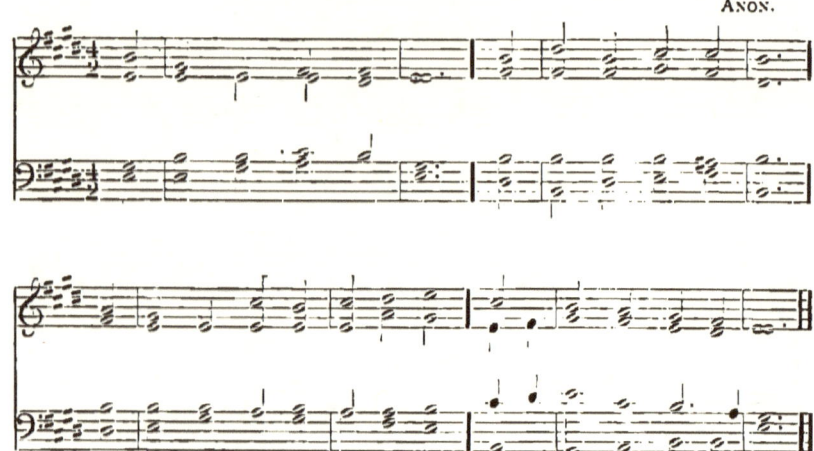

THIRD TUNE. S. M.

Sicily. 8s, 7s.

Sicilian Melody.

111

1
From the table now retiring,
  Which for us the Lord hath spread,
May our thought refreshment finding,
  Grow in all things like our Head!

2
His example while beholding,
  May our lives His image bear;
Him our Lord and Master calling,
  His commands may we revere.

3
Love to God and man displaying,
  Walking steadfast in His way,
Joy attend us in believing,
  Peace from God, through endless day.
        J. Rowe. *Alt. and Abr.*

112

1
Call the Lord thy sure salvation,
  Rest beneath the Almighty's shade;
In His secret habitation
  Dwell, nor ever be dismayed.

2
He shall charge His angel legions
  Watch and ward o'er thee to keep,
Though thou walk thro' hostile regions,
  Though in desert wilds thou sleep.

3
There no tumult can alarm thee,
  Thou shalt dread no hidden snare;
Guile nor violence shall harm thee
  In eternal safeguard there.
        James Montgomery. *Abr.*

CHRISTIAN SCIENCE HYMNAL. 113

SECOND TUNE. 8s, 7s.
Rev. J. B. Dykes, Mus. Doc.

THIRD TUNE. 8s, 7s.

Bartimeus. 8s, 7s.

STEPHEN JENKS.

113

Onward, Christian, though the region
  Where thou art be drear and lone;
God hath set a guardian legion
  Very near thee,— press thou on!

2
By the thorn-road, and none other,
  Is the mount of vision won;
Tread it without shrinking, brother!
  Jesus trod it,— press thou on!

3
By thy trustful, calm endeavor,
  Guiding, cheering, like the sun,
Earth-bound hearts thou shalt deliver;
  Oh, for their sake, press thou on!

S. JOHNSON. *Abr.*

114

1
God is love; His mercy brightens
  All the path in which we rove;
Bliss He wakes and woe He lightens;
  God is wisdom, God is love.

2
E'en the hour that darkest seemeth,
  Will His changeless goodness prove;
From the gloom His brightness streameth,
  God is wisdom, God is love.

3
He with earthly cares entwineth
  Hope and comfort from above:
Everywhere His glory shineth;
  God is wisdom, God is love.

BOWRING. *Abr.*

SECOND TUNE. 8s, 7s.

John Sebastian Bach. Arr. by Steggall.

THIRD TUNE. 8s, 7s.

The small notes are for accompaniment only.

 **Rathbun.** 8s, 7s.

I. Conkey.

115

1
Well for him who all things losing,
　E'en himself doth count as naught,
Still the one thing needful choosing,
　That with all true bliss is fraught!

2
Well for him who nothing knoweth
　But his God, whose boundless love
Makes the heart wherein it gloweth
　Calm and pure and faithful prove!

3
Well for him who all forsaking,
　Walketh not in shadows vain,
But the path of peace is taking
　Through this vale of tears and pain!

4
O that we our hearts might sever
　From earth's tempting vanities,
Fixing them on Him forever
　In whom all our fullness lies!

Gottfried Arnold. Tr. by Miss C. Winkworth.
Alt. and Abr.

116

1
Cast thy bread upon the waters,
　Thinking not 't is thrown away;
God Himself saith, thou shalt gather
　It again some future day.

2
Cast thy bread upon the waters;
　Wildly though the billows roll,
They but aid thee as thou toilest
　Truth to spread from pole to pole.

3
As the seed by billows floated,
　To some distant island lone,
So to human hearts benighted,
　That thou flingest may be borne.

J. H. Hanaford. Alt. and Abr.

SECOND TUNE. 8s, 7s.

WM. HENRY MONK, Mus. Doc.

THIRD TUNE. 8s, 7s.

Stockwell. 8s, 7s.

D. E. Jones.

117

1
Hear our prayer, oh gracious Father,
 Author of celestial good,
That Thy laws so pure and holy
 May be better understood.

2
Armed with faith may we press onward,
 Knowing nothing but Thy will,
Conquering every storm of error,
 With the sweet words, "Peace be still."

3
Like the star of Bethlehem shining,
 Love will guide us all the way,
From the depths of error's darkness,
 Into Truth's eternal day.

118

1
Know, O child, thy full salvation;
 Rise o'er sin and fear and care;
Joy to find, in every station,
 Something still to do, or bear.

2
Think what spirit dwells within thee;
 Think what Father's smiles are thine;
Think what Jesus did to win thee;
 Child of heaven, can'st thou repine?

3
Haste thee on from grace to glory,
 Arm'd with faith and wing'd with pray'r,
Heaven's eternal day before thee,
 God's own hand shall guide thee there.

Henry Francis Lyte. *Alt. and Abr.*

SECOND TUNE. 8s, 7s.
RICHARD REDHEAD.

THIRD TUNE. 8s, 7s.

Wilmot. 8s, 7s.
CARL MARIA VON WEBER.

119

1
On the night of that last supper,
Seated with His chosen band,
Christ, as food to all His brethren,
Gives Himself, with His own hand.

2
He, as man with man conversing,
Staid the seeds of truth to sow;
Then He closed, in solemn order,
Wondrously, His life of woe.

3
Lo! o'er ancient forms departing,
Newer rights of grace prevail;
Faith for all defects supplying,
Where the feeble senses fail.

4
To the everlasting Father,
Through the Son who reigns on high,
Be salvation, honor, blessing,
Might, and endless majesty.
BREVIARY.

120

1
Father, hear the prayer we offer:
Not for ease that prayer shall be;
But for strength, that we may ever
Live our lives courageously.

2
Not for ever in green pastures
Do we ask our way to be;
But the steep and rugged pathway
May we tread rejoicingly.

3
Not for ever by still waters
Would we idly quiet stay;
But would smite the living fountains
From the rocks along our way.
HYMNS OF THE SPIRIT. *Abr.*

SECOND TUNE. 8s, 7s.

Gothäer Cantional, 1715.

THIRD TUNE. 8s, 7s.

Science. 8s, 7s.

BRACKETT.

121

1
Now sweeping down the years untold,
  The day of Truth is breaking;
And sweet and fair the leaves unfold,
  Of Love's immortal waking.

2
For flower and fruitage now are seen,
  Where blight and mildew rested:
The Christ to-day to us, has been
  By word and deed attested.

3
His living presence we have felt—
  The "word made flesh" among us:
And hearts of stone before Him melt—
  His peace is brooding o'er us.
    LAURA C. NOURSE. *Alt. and Abr.*

122

1
With Love and Peace and Joy supreme,
  We hail the new appearing;
From out the darkness and the dream,
  The hav'n of rest is nearing.

2
For God is all; and Christ the way—
  Earth's meek and bold defender—
Has cleft the night, and lo! the day
  Bursts forth in mighty splendor.
    LAURA C. NOURSE. *Alt. and Abr.*

SECOND TUNE. 8s, 7s.

Rev. J. B. Dykes, Mus. Doc.

THIRD TUNE. 8s, 7s.

Bass (or Tenor Solo.)

ad lib.

The small notes are for accompaniment only.

St. Sylvester. 8s, 7s.

J. B. Dykes.

123

1
Theories, which thousands cherish,
　Pass like clouds that sweep the sky;
Creeds and dogmas all may perish;
　Truth Herself can never die.

2
Worldlings blindly may refuse Her,
　Close their eyes and call it night;
Learned scoffers may abuse Her,
　But they cannot quench Her light!

3
Thrones may totter, empires crumble,
　All their glories cease to be;
While She, Christ-like, crowns the humble,
　And from bondage sets them free.
　　　　　　　　Waterston. *Abr.*

124

1
Vainly, through night's weary hours,
　Keep we watch, lest foes alarm;
Vain our bulwarks, and our towers,
　But for God's protecting arm.

2
Vain were all our toil and labor,
　Did not God that labor bless;
Vain, without His grace and favor,
　Every talent we possess.

3
Vainer still the hope of heaven,
　That on human strength relies;
But to him shall help be given,
　Who in humble faith applies.
　　　　　　　　H. Auber. *Abr.*

SECOND TUNE. 8s, 7s.

Joachim Neander.

THIRD TUNE. 8s, 7s.

ritard

Autumn. 8s, 7s. D.

SPANISH MELODY. MARECHIO.

125

1

O, my people! journeying onward,—
  You of Christ's great brotherhood,
Heed the lessons which He gives you,
  Written in His blessed word
Strong and clear and full of meaning:
  Come, if you would follow Me.
Down among the poor and lowly;
  Here your Christian work must be.

2

This the path which you must follow,
  This the way the Saviour trod;
And He teaches this will lead you
  Into peace and up to God.
'Tis in deeds we serve the Master.—
  Words are idle, empty prayer;
All our Christian life a pretense,
  If the deeds are wanting there.

3

If you will but heed this lesson,
  Which the blessed Saviour gave,
Going out into the by-ways
  Seeking those He came to save,
Telling them the wondrous story,
  With an earnest heart of love,—
Yours will be a glorious harvest
  Gathered for the fold above.

Mrs. F. S. LOVEJOY.

126

1

True, the heart grows rich in giving;
  All its wealth is living grain;
Seeds which mildew in the garner,
  Scattered, fill with gold the plain.
Is thy burden hard and heavy?
  Do thy steps drag wearily?
Help to bear thy brother's burden,
  God will bear both it and thee.

2

Is the heart a well left empty?
  None but God its void can fill;
Nothing but a ceaseless Fountain
  Can its ceaseless longings still.
Is the heart a living power?
  Self-entwined, its strength sinks low,
It can only live in loving,
  And by serving love will grow.

ELIZABETH CHARLES. *Alt. and Abr.*

SECOND TUNE. 8s, 7s. D.

F. J. Haydn.

THIRD TUNE. 8s, 7s. D.

The small notes are for accompaniment only.

Bavaria. 8s, 7s. D.

GERMAN.

127

1
Breaking through the clouds of darkness,
　Black with error, doubt and fear;
Lighting up each sombre shadow,
　With a radiance soft and clear;
Filling every heart with gladness,
　That its holy power feels,
Comes the Christian Science Gospel;
　Sin it kills and grief it heals.

2
Christlike in its benedictions,
　Godlike in its strength sublime,
Conquering every subtle error,
　With a meekness all divine,—
May it go across the ocean,
　And be known in every land,
Till our sisters and our brothers,
　Are united in one band.

F. L. HEYWOOD. *Alt. and Abr.*

128

1
Peace be to this congregation!
　Peace to every heart therein!
Peace, the earnest of salvation;
　Peace, the fruit of conquered sin;
Peace, that speaks the heavenly Giver;
　Peace, to worldly minds unknown;
Peace, that floweth, as a river,
　From th'eternal Source alone.

2
O thou God of Peace, be near us,
　Fix within our hearts Thy home;
With Thy bright appearing cheer us,
　In Thy blesséd freedom come.
Come with all Thy revelations,
　Truth which we so long have sought;
Come with Thy deep consolations,
　Peace of God which passeth thought!

WESLEYAN.

SECOND TUNE. 8s, 7s. D.

HENRY SMART.

THIRD TUNE. 8s, 7s. D.

ALL VOICES IN UNISON.

The small notes are for accompaniment only.

Greenville. 8s, 7s. D. ROSSEAU.

129

1
Holy Father, Thou hast taught us
  We should live to Thee alone;
Year by year, Thy hand hath brought us
  On through dangers oft unknown.
When we wandered, Thou hast found us;
  When we doubted, sent us light;
Still Thine arm has been around us,
  All our paths were in Thy sight.

2
We would trust in Thy protecting,
  Wholly rest upon Thine arm,
Follow wholly Thy directing,
  Thou our only guard from harm!
Keep us from our own undoing,
  Help us turn to Thee when tried,
Still our strength in Thee renewing,
  Keep us ever at Thy side!

ANON. *Alt.*

130

1
He that goeth forth with weeping,
  Bearing still the precious seed,
Never tiring, never sleeping,
  Soon shall see his toil succeed:
Showers of rain will fall from heaven,
  Then the cheering sun will shine,
So shall plenteous fruit be given,
  Through an influence all divine.

2
Sow thy seed, be never weary,
  Let not fear thy thoughts employ;
Though the prospect be most dreary,
  Thou may'st reap the fruits of joy:
Lo! the scene of verdure bright'ning,
  See the rising grain appear;
Look again! the fields are whit'ning,
  Harvest-time is surely near.

HASTINGS. *Alt.*

SECOND TUNE. 8s, 7s. D.

CHARLES HARFORD LLOYD, Mus. Bac.

THIRD TUNE. 8s, 7s. D.

The small notes are for accompaniment only.

132   CHRISTIAN SCIENCE HYMNAL.

Weimar. 8s, 7s, 4s.   Ancient Melody, 1648.

131

1
Look, ye saints! the day is breaking;
 Joyful times are near at hand;
God, the mighty God, is speaking
 By His word in every land:
  Day advances —
Darkness flees at His command.

2
God of Jacob, high and glorious!
 Let Thy people see Thy power;
Let the gospel be victorious
 Through the world for evermore:
  Then shall idols
Perish, while Thy saints adore.
                            Kelly. *Alt.*

132

1
Every human tie may perish;
 Friend to friend unfaithful prove;
Mothers cease their own to cherish;
 Heaven and earth at last remove;
  But no changes
Can attend Jehovah's love.

2
In the furnace God may prove thee,
 Thence to bring thee forth more bright,
But can never cease to love thee;
 Thou art precious in His sight:
  God is with thee,
God thine everlasting light.
                  Rev. Thomas Kelly. *Abr.*

SECOND TUNE. 8s, 7s, 4s.

William Henry Monk, Mus. Doc.

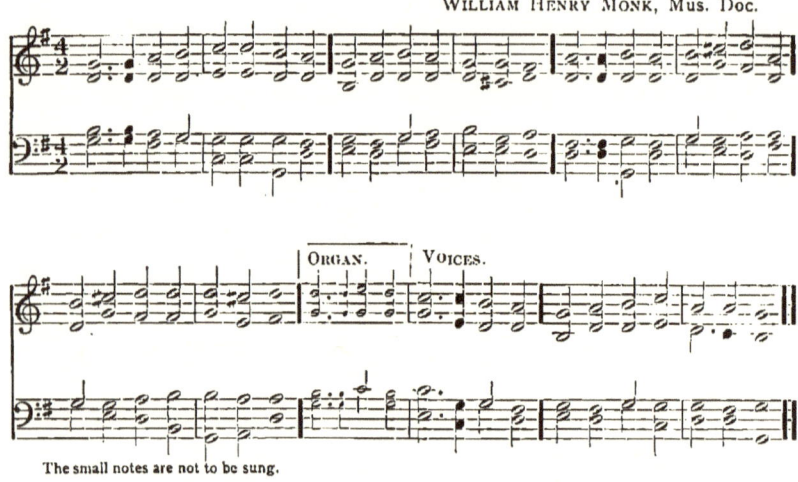

The small notes are not to be sung.

THIRD TUNE. 8s, 7s, 4s.

The small notes are not to be sung.

Zion. 8s, 7s, 4s.

THOMAS HASTINGS.

133

1
Come, Thou all-transforming Spirit,
  Bless the sower and the seed;
Let each heart Thy grace inherit;
  Raise the weak, the hungry feed!
    ‖: From the gospel
  Now supply Thy people's need. :‖

2
Oh, may all enjoy the blessing
  Which Thy word's designed to give;
Let us all, Thy love possessing,—
  Joyfully the truth receive;
    ‖: And forever
  To Thy praise and glory live. :‖
                              ANON.

134

1
Guide me, O Thou great Jehovah!
  Pilgrim through this barren land:
I am weak, but Thou art mighty;
  Hold me with Thy powerful hand.
    ‖: Bread of heaven!
  Feed me till I want no more. :‖

2
Open is the crystal fountain,
  Whence the healing waters flow:
And the fiery cloudy pillar
  Leads me all my journey through.
    ‖: Strong Deliverer!
  Still Thou art my strength and shield. :‖
               WILLIAM WILLIAMS. *Alt. and Abr.*

* When sung to the Second or Third Tune on opposite page, the last two lines of hymn are not repeated.

SECOND TUNE. 8s, 7s, 4s.
H. S. Irons.

THIRD TUNE. 8s, 7s, 4s.

Nuremberg. 7s.

JOHANN RUDOLPH AHLE.

135

1
Day by day the manna fell:
Oh, to learn this lesson well!
Still by constant mercy fed,
Give me, Lord, my daily bread.

2
Day by day the promise reads,
"Daily strength for daily needs:
Cast foreboding fears away;
Take the manna of to-day."

3
Lord, my times are in Thy hand:
All my sanguine hopes have planned,
To Thy wisdom I resign,
And would mould my will to Thine.

4
Thou my daily task shalt give;
Day by day to Thee I live;
So shall added years fulfil
Not my own, my Father's will.

JOSIAH CONDER.

136

1
Everlasting arms of Love
Are beneath, around, above;
God it is who bears us on,
His the arm we lean upon.

2
He our ever-present Guide
Faithful is, whate'er betide;
Gladly, then, we journey on,
With His arm to lean upon.

ANON.

SECOND TUNE. 7s.

J. H. Knecht.

THIRD TUNE. 7s.

 7s.

C. H. A. MALAN.

137

1
Mighty God, the First, the Last,
 What are ages in Thy sight
But as yesterday when past.
 ‖: Or a watch within the night? :‖

2
All that being e'er shall know,
 On, still on, through farthest years,
All eternity can show,
 ‖: Bright before Thee now appears. :‖

3
Whatsoe'er our lot may be,
 Calmly in this thought we'll rest,—
When we see as Thou dost see,
 ‖: We shall love Thee and be blest. :‖
    WILLIAM GASKELL. *Abr. and Alt.*

138

1
Partners of a glorious hope!
 Lift your hearts and voices up;
Nobly let us bear the strife,
 ‖: Keep the holiness of life; :‖

2
Still forget the things behind,
 Follow God the only Mind,
To the mark unwearied press,
 ‖: Seize the crown of righteousness. :‖

3
In our lives our faith be known,
 Faith by holy actions shown;
Faith that mountains can remove,
 ‖: Faith that always works by love. :‖
            WESLEYAN. *Alt.*

SECOND TUNE. 7s.

H. J. GAUNTLETT. Mus. Doc.

THIRD TUNE. 7s.

The small notes are for accompaniment only.

 **Pleyel.** 7s.

IGNACE PLEYEL.

139

1
Word of Life, most pure, most strong!
Lo! for thee the nations long;
Spread, till from its dreary night
All the world awakes to light.

2
Lo! the ripening fields we see:
Mighty shall the harvest be;
But the reapers still are few;
Great the work they have to do.

3
Lord of harvest, let there be
Joy and strength to work for Thee,
Till the nations far and near
See Thy light, Thy law revere.

FROM THE GERMAN.

140

1
Wait, my heart, upon the Lord,
To His gracious promise flee,
Laying hold upon His word,
"As thy days thy strength shall be."

2
If the sorrows of thy case
Seem peculiar still to thee,
God has promised needful grace—
"As thy days thy strength shall be."

3
Rock of Ages, I'm secure,
With Thy promise full and free;
Faithful, positive, and sure—
"As thy days thy strength shall be."

W. F. LLOYD. *Alt. and Abr*

SECOND TUNE. 7s.

Sir John Stainer, M. A., Mus. Doc.

THIRD TUNE. 7s.

Dijon. 7s.

GERMAN EVENING HYMN.

141

1
They who seek the throne of grace,
Find that throne in every place:
If we live a life of prayer,
God is present everywhere.

2
In our sickness, in our health;
In our want, or in our wealth,
If we look to God in prayer,
God is present everywhere.

3
Then, my heart, in every strait,
To thy Father come and wait;
He will answer every prayer:
God is present everywhere.

ANON.

142

1
Holy Bible! book divine!
Precious treasure! thou art mine:
Mine to tell me whence I came;
Mine to tell me what I am;—

2
Mine to chide me when I rove,
Mine to show a Saviour's love;
Mine thou art to guide and guard;
Mine to give a rich reward;—

3
Mine to comfort in distress,
If the Holy Spirit bless;
Mine to show, by living faith,
Man can triumph over death;—

ANON. *Abr.*

SECOND TUNE. 7s.

Rev. J. B. Dykes, Mus. Doc.

THIRD TUNE. 7s.

Herford. 7s.

ENGLISH TUNE.

143

1

They are slaves who will not choose
Hatred, scoffing, and abuse,
Rather than, in silence, shrink
From the truth they needs must think.

2

They are slaves, who fear to speak
For the fallen and the weak;
They are slaves, who dare not be
In the right with two or three.

LOWELL.

144

1

God made all His creatures free;
Life itself is liberty;
God ordained no other bands
Than united hearts and hands.

2

So shall all our slavery cease,
All God's children dwell in peace,
And the new-born earth record
Love, and Love alone, is Lord.

MONTGOMERY. *Alt. and Abr.*

SECOND TUNE. 7s.

Myles B. Foster.

THIRD TUNE. 7s.

The small notes are for accompaniment only.

Halle. 7s. 6l.

F. J. Haydn.

145

1

Gracious spirit, dwell with me;
I myself would gracious be,
And, with words that help and heal,
Would thy life in mine reveal;
And with actions bold and meek
Christ's own gracious spirit speak.

2

Truthful spirit, dwell with me;
I myself would truthful be,
And with wisdom kind and clear
Let thy life in mine appear;
And with actions brotherly
Follow Christ's sincerity.

3

Mighty spirit, dwell with me;
I myself would mighty be,
Mighty so as to prevail
Where unaided man must fail;
Ever by a mighty hope
Pressing on and bearing up.

Thomas Toke Lynch, 1855. *Abr.*

SECOND TUNE. 7s. 6l.

Henry Smart.

THIRD TUNE. 7s. 6l.

Watchman. 7s. D.

LOWELL MASON.

146

1

Watchman, tell us of the night,
  What its signs of promise are?
Trav'ler, o'er yon mountain's height
  See that glory-beaming star!
Watchman, does its beauteous ray
  Aught of hope or joy foretell?
Trav'ler, yes; it brings the day,
  Promised day of Israel.

2

Watchman, tell us of the night;
  Higher yet that star ascends;
Trav'ler, blessedness and light,
  Peace and truth its course portends;
Watchman, will its beams alone
  Gild the spot that gave them birth?
Trav'ler, ages are its own;
  See, it bursts o'er all the earth!

3

Watchman, tell us of the night,
  For the morning seems to dawn;
Trav'ler, darkness takes its flight,
  Doubt and terror are withdrawn;
Watchman, let thy wand'rings cease;
  Hie thee to thy quiet home!
Trav'ler, lo! the Prince of peace,
  Lo! the Son of God, is come!

JOHN BOWRING. 1825.

SECOND TUNE. 7s. D.

Sir George J. Elvey, Mus. Doc.

THIRD TUNE. 7s. D.

Webb. 7s, 6s. D. G. J. Webb.

147

1
The morning light is breaking;
 The darkness disappears!
The sons of earth are waking
 To penitential tears;
Each breeze that sweeps the ocean
 Brings tidings from afar,
Of nations in commotion,
 Prepared for Zion's war.

2
Blest river of salvation!
 Pursue thine onward way;
Flow thou to every nation,
 Nor in thy richness stay:
Stay not till all the lowly
 Triumphant reach their home:
Stay not till all the holy
 Proclaim—"The Lord is come!"
　　　　　　　　S. F. Smith.

148

1
God comes, with succor speedy,
 To those who suffer wrong;
To help the poor and needy,
 And bid the weak be strong:
He comes to break oppression,
 And set the captive free.
To take away transgression,
 And rule in equity.

2
To Him shall prayer unceasing,
 And daily vows, ascend;
His kingdom still increasing,
 A kingdom without end.
The tide of time shall never
 His covenant remove;
His name shall stand forever;
 His great, best name of Love.
　　　　　　　James Montgomery. *Abr*

SECOND TUNE. 7s, 6s. D.

S. S. WESLEY, Mus. Doc.

THIRD TUNE. 7s, 6s. D.

TENOR SOLO.

Ewing. 7s, 6s. D.

ALEXANDER EWING.

149

1
In heavenly love abiding,
 No change my heart shall fear;
And safe is such confiding,
 For nothing changes here.
The storm may roar without me,
 My heart may low be laid;
But God is round about me,
 And can I be dismayed?

2
Wherever He may guide me,
 No want shall turn me back;
My shepherd is beside me,
 And nothing can I lack.
His wisdom ever waketh,
 His sight is never dim;
He knows the way He taketh,
 And I will walk with Him.

3
Green pastures are before me,
 Which yet I have not seen;
Bright skies will soon be o'er me
 Where darkest clouds have been.

My hope I cannot measure,
 My path in life is free:
My Father has my treasure,
 And He will walk with me.
 ANNA L. WARING. 1850.

150

1
Now is the time approaching,
 By prophets long foretold,
When all shall dwell together,
 One shepherd and one fold.
Now Jew and Gentile, meeting
 From many a distant shore,
Around one altar kneeling,
 One common Lord adore.

2
Let all that now divides us
 Remove and pass away,
Like shadows of the morning
 Before the blaze of day.
Let all that now unites us
 More sweet and lasting prove,
A closer bond of union,
 In a blest land of love.
 JANE BORTWICK. *Abr*

CHRISTIAN SCIENCE HYMNAL. 153

SECOND TUNE. 7s, 6s. D.
J. W. ELLIOTT.

The small notes are for accompaniment only.

THIRD TUNE. 7s, 6s. D.

The small notes are for accompaniment only.

Greenland. 7s, 6s. D.

LAUSANNE PSALTER.

151

1
How beauteous on the mountains,
  The feet of him that brings,
Like streams from living fountains,
  Good tidings of good things;
That publisheth salvation,
  And jubilee release,
To every tribe and nation,
  God's reign of joy and peace!

2
Break forth in hymns of gladness;
  O waste Jerusalem!
Let songs, instead of sadness,
  Thy jubilee proclaim;
The Lord, in strength victorious,
  Upon thy foes hath trod;
Behold, O earth! the glorious
  Salvation of our God!

B. GOUGH. *Abr.*

152

1
God is my strong salvation;
  What foe have I to fear?
In darkness and temptation,
  My Light, my Help is near:
Though hosts encamp around me,
  Firm in the fight I stand;
What terror can confound me,
  With God at my right hand?

2
Place on the Lord reliance;
  My heart, with courage wait;
His truth be thine alliance,
  When faint and desolate:
His might thy heart shall strengthen,
  His love thy joy increase;
Mercy thy day shall lengthen;
  The Lord will give thee peace!

JAMES MONTGOMERY.

CHRISTIAN SCIENCE HYMNAL. 155

SECOND TUNE. 7s, 6s. D.

Sir John Stainer, M. A., Mus. Doc.

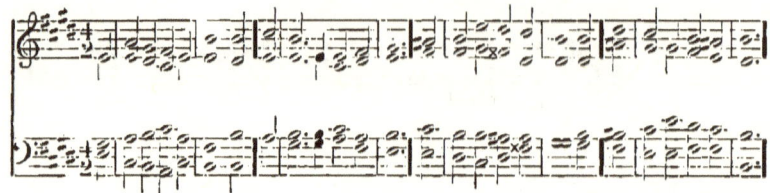

THIRD TUNE. 7s, 6s. D.

Missionary Hymn. 7s, 6s. D.

LOWELL MASON.

153

1
A glorious day is dawning,
 And o'er the waking earth
The heralds of the morning
 Are springing into birth.
In dark and hidden places
 There shines the blessèd light;
The beam of truth displaces
 The darkness of the night.

2
The advocates of error,
 Foresee the glorious morn,
And hear in shrinking terror,
 The watchword of reform.
It rings from hill and valley,
 It breaks oppression's chain,
A thousand freemen rally,
 And swell the mighty strain.

3
The watchword has been spoken,
 The light has broken forth,
Far shines the blessèd token
 Upon the startled earth.
To hearts and homes benighted
 The blessèd truth is given,
And peace and love, united,
 Point upward unto heaven.

154

1
I know no life divided,
 O Lord of life, from Thee;
In Thee is life provided
 For all mankind and me:
I know no death, O Father,
 Because I live in Thee;
Thy life it is which frees us
 From death eternally.

2
I fear no tribulation,
 Since, whatsoe'er it be,
It makes no separation
 Between my Lord and me.
Since Thou, my God and Teacher,
 Vouchsafe to be my own,
Though poor, I shall be richer
 Than monarch on his throne.

Rev. CARL JOHANN PHILIPP SPITTA.
Tr. by RICHARD MASSIE. *Alt. and Abr.*

SECOND TUNE. 7s, 6s. D.

WILLIAM HENRY MONK, Mus. Doc.

THIRD TUNE. 7s, 6s. D.

The small notes are for accompaniment only.

St. Cecilia. 6s.

Rev. L. G. HAYNE, Mus. Doc.

155

1
What is thy birthright, man,
  Child of the perfect One!
What is thy Father's plan
  For His belovèd son?

2
Thou art Truth's honest child,
  Sinless and pure of heart.
Treading, meek, undefiled
  In th'Master's steps apart.

3
Dreams of sense disappear
  As Truth dawns on the sight,
The phantoms of thy fear,
  Fleeing before the light.

4
Take then the charmèd rod;
  Thou art not error's thrall!
Thou hast the gift from God—
  Dominion over all.

      KATHLEEN. *Alt. and Abr.*

156

1
If God is all in all,
  His children cannot fear.
See baseless evil fall,
  Knowing that God is here!

2
If God is all, in space
  No subtle error creeps.
We see Truth's glowing face,
  And Love that never sleeps.

3
We see creative Mind,
  The Principle, the Life;
And Soul and Substance find,
  But never discord, strife.

4
Oh, Perfect and Divine!
  We hear Thy loving call,
And seek no earthly shrine
  But "crown Thee Lord of All."

      KATHLEEN. *Alt. and Abr.*

SECOND TUNE. 6s.

HENRY SMART.

THIRD TUNE. 6s.

a little slower.

St. Gertrude. 6s, 5s.

ARTHUR S. SULLIVAN.

157

1
Onward, Christian soldiers,
  Marching as to war,
With the cross of Jesus
  Going on before.
Christ, the royal Master,
  Leads against the foe;
Forward into battle,
  See, his banners go.

CHORUS.
Onward, Christian soldiers,
  Marching as to war,
With the cross of Jesus,
  Going on before.

2
Like a mighty army,
  Moves the Church of God;
Brothers, we are treading
  Where the saints have trod;
We are not divided,
  All one body we,
One in hope and doctrine,
  One in charity.   Cho.

3
Crowns and thrones may perish,
  Kingdoms rise and wane,
But the Church of Jesus
  Constant will remain;
Gates of hell can never
  'Gainst that Church prevail;
We have Christ's own promise,
  And that cannot fail.   Cho.

4
Onward, then, ye people,
  Join our happy throng;
Blend with ours your voices
  In the triumph-song;
Glory, laud, and honor
  Unto Christ the King;
This through countless ages,
  Men and angels sing.   Cho.

S. BARING-GOULD.

CHRISTIAN SCIENCE HYMNAL.

SECOND TUNE. 6s, 5s.
(HAYDN.) DR. DYKES.

THIRD TUNE. 6s, 5s.

The small notes are for accompaniment only.

Bethany. 6s, 4s.   LOWELL MASON.

158

1
Nearer, my God, to Thee, nearer to Thee:
E'en though it be a cross that raiseth me,
Still all my song shall be,—
Nearer, my God, to Thee.
Nearer, my God, to Thee, nearer to Thee.

2
Though like the wanderer, the sun gone down,
Darkness comes over me, my rest a stone,
Yet in my dreams I'd be
Nearer, my God, to Thee,
Nearer, my God, to Thee, nearer to Thee.

3
There let the way appear steps unto heav'n;
All that Thou sendest me in mercy given;
Angels to beckon me
Nearer, my God, to Thee.
Nearer, my God, to Thee, nearer to Thee.

4
Then, with my waking thoughts bright with Thy praise,
Out of my stony griefs Bethel I'll raise;
So by my woes to be
Nearer, my God, to Thee.
Nearer, my God, to Thee, nearer to Thee.

5
Or if on joyful wing cleaving the sky,
Sun, moon, and stars forgot, upwards I fly,
Still all my song shall be,
Nearer, my God, to Thee,
Nearer, my God, to Thee, nearer to Thee.

SARAH F. ADAMS.

SECOND TUNE. 6s, 4s.

Rev. J. B. Dykes, Mus. Doc.

THIRD TUNE. 6s, 4s.

The small notes are to be sung, but very softly.

Italian Hymn. 6s, 4s.

F. Giardini.

159

1
From out the hideous night,
Seeking Thy perfect light,
　Dear Lord, I come!
Ambushed on ev'ry side,
Dark error's foemen hide;
Ambushed on ev'ry side,
　Thou lead'st me on.

2
Armed with Thy Truth's sharp steel,
No fear of foes I feel,—
　Strong in Thy might.
Love, crowning all with peace,
Bids strife and tumult cease;
Love, crowning all with peace,
　Makes service light.

3
Turning from death and sin,
Thy Life to enter in,
　Lord, may I prove,—
All things to us are giv'n,
Health, hope, and joys of heaven,—
All things to us are giv'n,
　Gifts of Thy love.

M. M. *Alt.*

160

1
Truth comes alike to all,
Who on Her name dare call,
　With motives pure;
Then let us all unite,
With Freedom's star in sight,
Press onward in the right,
　Which shall endure.

2
Come, all-pervading Love,
Blest heart of Heaven above,
　O Spirit blest!
Life, Truth, and Good shall be
Our glorious Trinity.
And ev'ry heart shall see
　Eternal rest.

CHRISTIAN SCIENCE HYMNAL.

SECOND TUNE. 6s, 4s.

Rev. J. B. Dykes, Mus. Doc.

The small notes are for accompaniment only.

THIRD TUNE. 6s, 4s.

St. Nicolas. 7s, 5s. D.

W. STEVENSON HOYTE. *Alt.*

161

1
Shepherd, show me how to go
  O'er the hillside steep,
How to gather, how to sow,
  How to feed Thy sheep;
I will listen for Thy voice,
  Lest my footsteps stray,
I will follow and rejoice
  All the rugged way.

2
Thou wilt bind the stubborn will,
  Wound the callous breast,
Make self righteousness be still,
  Break earth's stupid rest;

Strangers on a barren shore
  Lab'ring long and lone—
We would enter by the door,
  And Thou know'st Thine own;

3
So when day grows dark and cold,
  Tear or triumph harms,
Lead Thy lambkins to the fold,
  Take them in Thine arms;
Feed the hungry, heal the heart,
  Till the morning's beam;
White as wool, ere they depart—
  Shepherd, wash them clean.

Rev MARY B. G. EDDY.

SECOND TUNE. 7s, 5s. D.

Sir G. A. MacFarren, Mus. Doc.

THIRD TUNE. 7s, 5s. D.

Vesper. 7, 7, 7, 3.

Sir John Stainer, M. A., Mus. Doc.

162

1
Gird thy heavenly armor on,
  Wear it ever night and day;
  Ambushed lies the evil one:
    Watch and pray.

2
Hear the victors who o'ercame;
  Still they mark each warrior's way
  All with warning voice exclaim,—
    Watch and pray.

3
Hear, above all, hear thy Lord;
  Him thou lovest to obey;
  Hide within thy heart his word,—
    Watch and pray.

Charlotte Elliott. *Abr.*
From "Geistliche Lieder."

SECOND TUNE. 7, 7, 7, 3.

JOSEPH BARNBY.

THIRD TUNE. 7, 7, 7, 3.

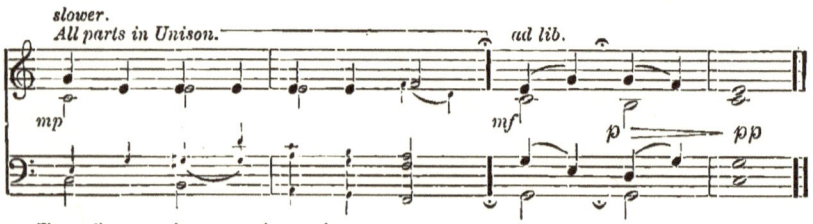

The small notes are for accompaniment only.

 8s, 4s. BRACKETT.

163

1
O'er waiting harpstrings of the mind
  There sweeps a strain,
Low, sad, and sweet, whose measures bind
  The power of pain;

2
And wake a white-winged angel throng
  Of thoughts, illumed
By faith, and breathed in raptured song,
  With love perfumed.

3
Then His unveiled, sweet mercies show
  Life's burdens light.
I kiss the cross, and wait to know
  A world more bright.

4
And o'er earth's troubled, angry sea
  I see Christ walk,
And come to me, and tenderly,
  Divinely talk.

5
Thus Truth engrounds me on the Rock
  Upon Life's shore,
'Gainst which the winds and waves can shock,
  Oh, nevermore!

6
From tired joy and grief afar,
  And nearer Thee,—
Father, where Thine own children are,
  I love to be.

7
My prayer, some daily good to do
  To Thine, for Thee,—
An offering pure of Love, whereto
  God leadeth me.

Rev. MARY BAKER G. EDDY.

Copyright, 1887. By permission.

SECOND TUNE. 8s, 4s.
William Henry Monk, Mus. Doc.

THIRD TUNE. 8s, 4s.

St. Vincent. 9s, 8s.

J. Uglow.

164

1
In Thee, oh Spirit, true and tender,
　I find my Life, as God's own child;
Within Thy Light of glorious splendor,
　I lose the earth-clouds, drear and wild.

2
Within Thy Love is safe abiding
　From every thought that giveth fear;
Within Thy Truth, a perfect chiding,
　Should I forget that Thou art near.

3
In Thee I have no pain or sorrow,
　No anxious thought, no load of care.
Thou art the same to-day, to-morrow;
　Thy Love and Truth are everywhere.

　　　　　　　　　　　F. A. F. *Abr.*

SECOND TUNE. 9s, 8s.

Dr. J. S. B. HODGES.

THIRD TUNE. 9s, 8s.

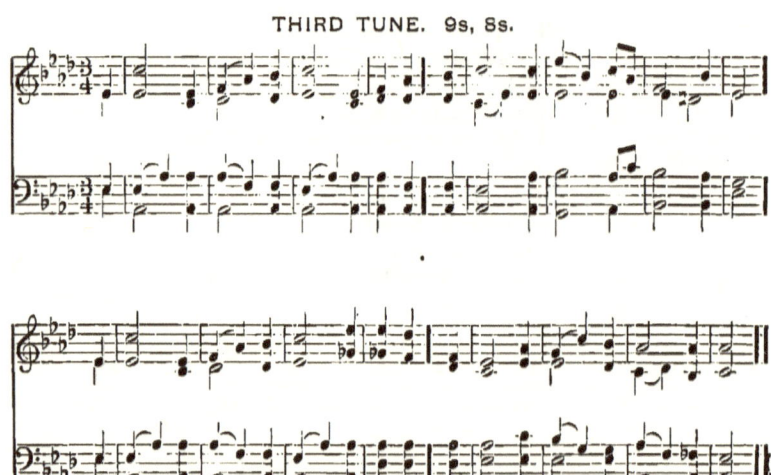

165

1
Abide with me: fast falls the eventide;
The darkness deepens; Lord, with me abide:
When other helpers fail, and comforts flee,
Help of the helpless, O abide with me.

2
I need Thy presence every passing hour.
What but Thy grace can foil the tempter's power?
Who like Thyself my guide and stay can be?
Through cloud and sunshine, O abide with me!

3
I fear no foe, with Thee at hand to bless;
Ills have no weight, and tears no bitterness:
Where is death's sting? where, grave, thy victory?
I triumph still, if Thou abide with me.

HENRY FRANCIS LYTE. *Abr.*

SECOND TUNE. 10s.
Henry Smart.

THIRD TUNE. 10s.

Redemptor. 10s.

ARTHUR HENRY BROWN.

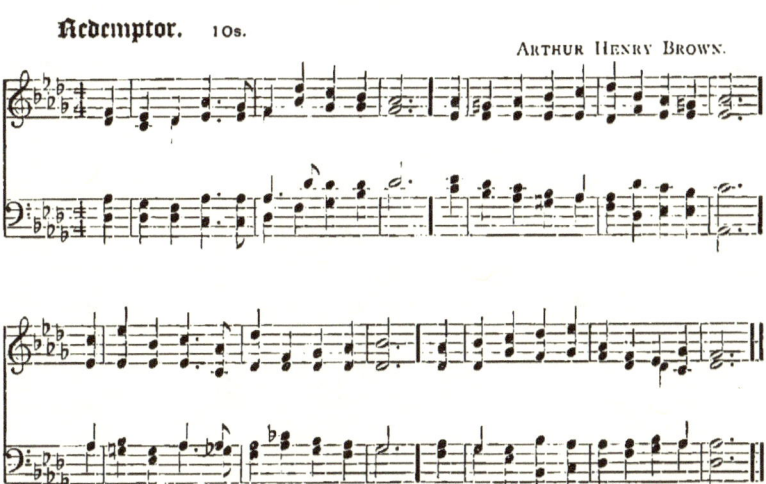

166

1
Here, O my Lord, I'd see Thee face to face;
　Here would I touch and handle things unseen;
　Here grasp with firmer hand th' eternal grace,
　And all my weariness upon Thee lean.

2
Here would I feed upon the bread of God;
　Here drink with Thee the royal wine of heav'n;
　Here would I lay aside each earthly load,
　Here taste afresh the calm of sin forgiv'n.

3
And as we rise, the symbols disappear;
　The feast, though not the love, is pass'd and gone;
　The bread and wine remove, but Thou art here —
　Nearer than ever — still my Shield and Sun.

4
Feast after feast thus comes and passes by;
　Yet, passing, points to the glad feast above —
　Giving sweet foretaste of the festal joy,
　The Lamb's great bridal feast of bliss and love.

HORATIUS BONAR. *Alt.*

CHRISTIAN SCIENCE HYMNAL. 177

SECOND TUNE. 10s.
WILLIAM HENRY MONK, Mus. Doc.

THIRD TUNE. 10s.

Berlin. 10s.

MENDELSSOHN.

167

1
Why is thy faith, O child of God, so small?
Why doth thy heart shrink back at duty's call?
Art thou obeying this—"Abide in me,"
And doth the Master's word abide in thee?

2
Oh, blest assurance from our risen Lord!
Oh, precious comfort breathing from the Word!
How great the promise! could there greater be?
"Ask what thou wilt, it shall be done for thee!"

3
"Ask what thou wilt," but, oh, remember this,—
We ask and have not, for we ask amiss
When, weak in faith, we only half believe
That what we ask we really shall receive.

W. F. SHERWIN. *Abr.*

SECOND TUNE. 10s.

WILLIAM HENRY MONK, Mus. Doc.

THIRD TUNE. 10s.

Truth. 10s.

I. PLEYEL.

168

1
O Thou great Friend to all the sons of men,
Who once appeared in humblest guise below,
Sin to rebuke, to break the captive's chain,
And call thy brethren forth from want and woe!

2
We look to thee; thy truth is still the light
Which guides the nations, groping on their way,
Stumbling and falling in disastrous night,
Yet hoping ever for the perfect day.

3
Yes: thou art still the Life; thou art the Way
The holiest know, — Light, Life, and Way of heaven;
And they who dearest hope, and deepest pray,
Toil, by the Light, Life, Way, which thou hast given.

THEODORE PARKER.

CHRISTIAN SCIENCE HYMNAL. 181

SECOND TUNE. 10s.

Everard Hulton, Mus. Bac.

THIRD TUNE. 10s.

Lux Benigna. 10, 4, 10, 4, 10, 10.

Rev. J. B. Dykes, Mus. Doc.

169

1
Lead, kindly Light, amid the encircling gloom,
  Lead Thou me on!
The night is dark, and I am far from home,—
  Lead Thou me on!
Keep Thou my feet! I do not ask to see
The distant scene,— one step enough for me.

2
I was not ever thus, nor prayed that Thou
  Shouldst lead me on:
I loved to choose and see my path; but now,
  Lead Thou me on!
I loved the garish day, and, spite of fears,
Pride ruled my will: remember not past years.
           JOHN HENRY NEWMAN. *Abr.*

SECOND TUNE. 10, 4, 10, 4, 10, 10.
Arranged from R. WAINWRIGHT, Mus. Doc.

THIRD TUNE. 10, 4, 10, 4, 10, 10.

Portuguese Hymn. 11s.

JOHN READING.

170

1
How firm a foundation, ye saints of the Lord!
Is laid for your faith in His excellent word!
What more can He say, than to you He hath said,—
To you, who for refuge to Jesus have fled?

2
"Fear not, I am with thee, oh, be not dismayed
For I am thy God, I will still give thee aid;
I'll strengthen thee, help thee, and cause thee to stand,
Upheld by My gracious, omnipotent hand.

3
"When through fiery trials thy pathway shall lie,
My grace, all-sufficient, shall be thy supply;
The flame shall not hurt thee; I only design
Thy dross to consume, and thy gold to refine."

G. KEITH. *Abr.*

Henley. 11s, 10s.

LOWELL MASON.

171

1
Still, still with Thee when purple morning breaketh,
When the tired waketh, and the shadows flee,
Fairer than morning, lovelier than the daylight,
Dawns the sweet consciousness, I am with Thee.

2
Alone with Thee, amid the seeming shadows,
The solemn hush of being, newly born,
Alone with Thee, in breathless adoration,
In the calm dew and freshness of the morn.

3
So shall it ever be in that bright morning,
When Divine sense bids every shadow flee,
And in that hour, fairer than daylight dawning,
Remains the glorious thought, I am with Thee.

HARRIET BEECHER STOWE. *Alt.*

172

1
Oh; he whom Jesus loved has truly spoken
That holier worship, which God deigns to bless,
Restores the lost, and heals the spirit-broken,
And feeds the widow and the fatherless.

2
Then, brother man, fold to thy heart thy brother!
For where love dwells, the peace of God is there:
To worship rightly is to love each other;
Each smile a hymn, each kindly deed a prayer.

3
Follow, with reverent steps, the great example
Of him whose holy work was doing good;
So shall the wide earth seem our Father's temple,
Each loving life a psalm of gratitude.

JOHN G. WHITTIER

SECOND TUNE. 11s, 10s.

Rev. J. B. Dykes, Mus. Doc.

THIRD TUNE. 11s, 10s.

173

1
Be firm and be faithful; desert not the right;
The brave become bolder the darker the night!
Then up and be doing, though cowards may fail;
Thy duty pursuing, dare all and prevail!

2
If scorn be thy portion, if hatred and loss,
If stripes or a prison, remember the cross!
God watches above thee, and He will requite;
Desert those that love thee, but never the right.

ANON.

174

1
While Thou, O my God, art my help and defender,
  No cares can o'erwhelm me, no terrors appall;
The wiles and the snares of this world will but render
  More lively my hopes in my God and my all.

2
Yes, Thou art my refuge in sorrow and danger,
  My strength when I suffer, my hope when I fall,
My comfort and joy in this land of the stranger,
  My treasure, my glory, my God, and my all.

SECOND TUNE. 11s, (or 12s, 11s.)

Arr. from CHARLES E. STEPHENS.

THIRD TUNE. 11s, (or 12s, 11s.)

Lischer. H. M.

F. Schneider.

175

1
My feet shall never slide,
Nor fall in fatal snares,
Since God, my guard and guide,
Defends me from my fears:
Those wakeful eyes | Shall Israel keep
That never sleep, | When dangers rise.

2
No burning heats by day,
Nor blasts of evening air,
Shall take my health away,
For God is with me there:
Thou art my sun, | To guard my head
And Thou my shade, | By night or noon.

WATTS. *Alt. and Abr.*

SECOND TUNE. H. M.

Sir John Stainer, M. A., Mus. Doc.

THIRD TUNE. H. M.

The small notes are for accompaniment only.

Calm. 8, 6, 8, 6, 8, 8.

THOMAS HASTINGS.

176

1
I look to Thee in every need,
 And never look in vain;
I feel Thy touch, eternal Love,
 And all is well again:
The thought of Thee is mightier far
Than sin and pain and sorrow are.

2
Discouraged in the work of life,
 Disheartened by its load,
Shamed by its failures or its fears,
 I sink beside the road;
But let me only think of Thee,
And then new heart springs up in me.

3
Embosomed deep in Thy dear love,
 Held in Thy law, I stand;
Thy hand in all things I behold,
 And all things in Thy hand;
Thou leadest me by unsought ways,
And turn'st my mourning into praise.

SAMUEL LONGFELLOW. *Abr.*

177

1
Oh, be not faithless! with the morn
 Cast thou abroad thy grain!
At noon faint not, nor be forlorn,
 At evening sow again!
Blessèd are they, whate'er betide,
Who thus all waters sow beside.

2
Thou knowest not which seed shall grow,
 Or which may die or live;
In faith and hope, and patience, sow!
 The increase God shall give,
According to His gracious will,
As best His purpose may fulfill.

3
Oh, could our inward eye but view,
 Our hearts but feel aright,
What faith and love and hope can do,
 By their celestial might,
We should not say, with lonely dread,
The power of miracle is fled!

BERNARD BARTON. *Alt.*

CHRISTIAN SCIENCE HYMNAL.

SECOND TUNE. 8, 6, 8, 6, 8, 8.

E. J. Hopkins.

THIRD TUNE. 8, 6, 8, 6, 8, 8.

194　　CHRISTIAN SCIENCE HYMNAL.

Communion Hymn.　10, 7, 7, 7, 9.

BRACKETT.

178

1
Saw ye my Saviour? Heard ye the glad sound?
Felt ye the power of the Word?
'T was the truth that made us free,
And was found by you and me
In the life and the love of our Lord.

2
Mourner, it calls you—come to my bosom,
Love wipes your tears all away,
And will lift the shade of gloom,
And for you make radiant room
Midst the glories of one endless day.

3
Sinner, it calls you — come to this fountain;
Cleanse the foul senses within;
'T is the Spirit that makes pure,
That exalts thee, and will cure
All thy sorrow and sickness and sin.

4
Strongest deliverer, friend of the friendless,
Life of all Being divine:
Thou the Christ, and not the creed;
Thou the Truth, in thought and deed;
Thou the water, the bread, and the wine.

Rev. MARY BAKER. G. EDDY.

Copyright, 1889, by Rev. Mary B. G. Eddy. By permission.

179. Out of Self and Into Thee.

JESSIE H. BROWN.   J. H. F.

1. Out of sad-ness in-to glad-ness, Sav-iour, Thou hast bid-den me;
2. Out of ter-ror, out of er-ror, Out of all that dark-ness brings,
3. Out of seem-ing, out of dream-ing, Out of earth's un-cer-tain-ty,

In-to bless-ing, all pos-sess-ing, Out of self and in-to Thee.
In-to un-ion and com-mun-ion With the ho-ly King of kings.
In-to sure-ness and se-cure-ness— Out of self and in-to Thee.

REFRAIN.

Out of self and in-to Thee! Lord, thy won-drous love I see; Let me dai-ly far-ther flee, Out of self and in-to Thee.

Copyright, 1894, by Fillmore Bros. By permission.

181. The Light of the World.*

Let your light so shine before men.—MATT. 5: 16.

D. R. LUCAS.   CHAS. M. FILLMORE.

1. The light of the world you must be, T'en-light-en and res-cue man-kind, That
2. The light of the world, may your life Trans-par-ent with ex-cel-lence shine, A re-
3. The light of the world, ev-'ry day Let your light on your fel-low-men shine, That be-

they your ex - am - ple may see, Of wis-dom and vir - tue com - bined.
proach to cor - rup-tion and strife, As you fol-low the Sav-iour di - vine.
hold - ing your up - rightness, they By your works to the good may in - cline.

CHORUS.

The light of the world, . . The light of the world! The
The light of the world you must be, The light of the world you must be;
                                             you must be,

light of the world you must be, . . That all your ex - am - ple may see.

*Abr.

Copyright, 1886, by Fillmore Bros. By permission.

182 These Sayings of Mine.

A. P. COBB. CHAS. EDW. PRIOR.

1. Who-so hear-eth and do-eth "these say-ings of mine,"
2. Who-so hear-eth and scorn-eth "these say-ings of mine,"
3. Art thou fool-ish or wise, O, broth-er of mine?

I will lik-en to one, who thro' storm and thro' shine,
Is fool-ish-ly build-ing thro' storm and thro' shine,
Art thou heed-ing thy Sav-iour, thro' storm and thro' shine?

His house wise-ly builds on the firm rock be-low,
His house on the sand, and 'twill speed-i-ly fall,
On the rock or the sand, oh, tell me, I pray,

And safe there a-bides, when the fierce tem-pests blow.
When the rain shall de-scend, and the tem-pest shall fall.
On which art thou build-ing thy dwell-ing each day?

Copyright, 1887, by E. O. Excell. By permission.

CHRISTIAN SCIENCE HYMNAL. 201

184 Christ for the World we sing.

Rev. S. Wolcott, D.D.   (CUTTING.)   Wm. F. Sherwin, by per.

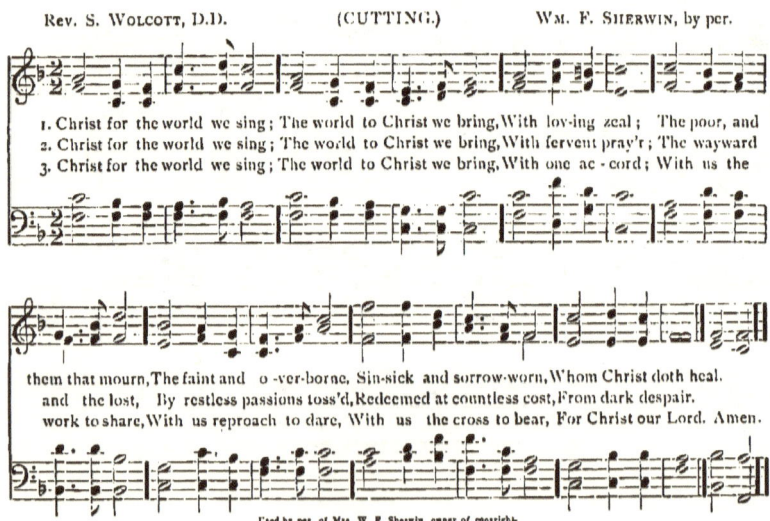

1. Christ for the world we sing; The world to Christ we bring, With lov-ing zeal; The poor, and
2. Christ for the world we sing; The world to Christ we bring, With fervent pray'r; The wayward
3. Christ for the world we sing; The world to Christ we bring, With one ac-cord; With us the

them that mourn, The faint and o-ver-borne, Sin-sick and sorrow-worn, Whom Christ doth heal.
and the lost, By restless passions toss'd, Redeemed at countless cost, From dark despair.
work to share, With us reproach to dare, With us the cross to bear, For Christ our Lord. Amen.

Used by per. of Mrs. W. F. Sherwin, owner of copyright.

185 Rouse, ye Soldiers!

Watch ye, stand fast in the faith, quit you like men, be strong. — 1 COR. 16: 13.

M. H. TIPTON.   J. H. F.

Earnestly.

1. Rouse, ye sol-diers of the cross! And put your ar-mor on;
2. Rouse, ye sol-diers brave and true! Un-furl your ban-ner high!
3. Rouse, ye sol-diers, to the charge! Our Cap-tain's gone be-fore;

Brave-ly fight for truth and right, Till vic-to-ry is won.
Bold-ly stand at Christ's command, For, see, the foe is nigh!
Grand-ly march with shout and song, Un-til the war is o'er.

CHORUS.

Rouse ye! Rouse ye! Rouse ye, soldiers, brave and strong, brave and strong, Bold-ly fight for the truth and right, And win the vic-tor's crown, crown.

Copyright, 1891 by Fillmore Bros. By permission.

186. Blessed are the Poor in Spirit.

Matt. 5: 3.

D. R. L.
Not too fast.

J. H. F.

1. Bless-ed they in spir-it poor, Not ex-alt-ed by their pride,
2. Bless-ed those in spir-it poor, For the Lord to them has giv'n,

Knock-ing at the kingdom's door, Seek-ing Christ, what-e'er be-tide;
Pre-cious prom-ise that be-fore Comes to them the reign of Heav'n;

Well con-vinced that he will sure, All his prom-is-es ful-fill,
'Tis their own in-her-i-tance, Here on earth and ev-er-more,

Keep-ing them in faith se-cure, Who o-bey his ho-ly will.
For to them he free-ly grants All the king-dom's bless-ed store.

Copyright, 1891, by Fillmore Bros. By permission.

to the throne of God shall stand the pure in heart.

190 Blessed are the Peacemakers.

MATT. 5: 9.

D. R. L. J. H. F.

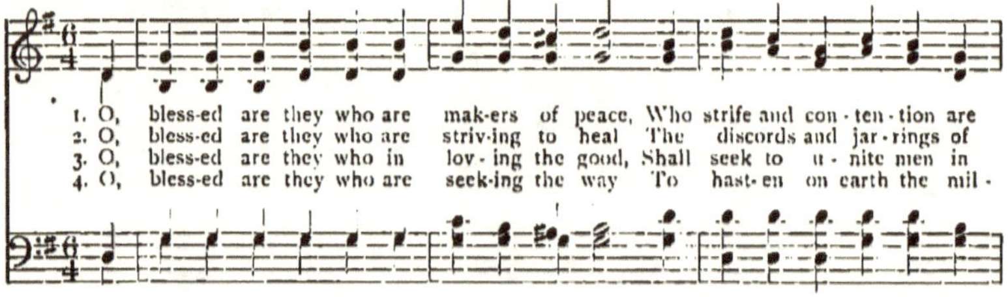

1. O, bless-ed are they who are mak-ers of peace, Who strife and con-ten-tion are
2. O, bless-ed are they who are striv-ing to heal The discords and jar-rings of
3. O, bless-ed are they who in lov-ing the good, Shall seek to u-nite men in
4. O, bless-ed are they who are seek-ing the way To hast-en on earth the mil-

caus - ing to cease, Who, walk-ing in love, the true path-way have trod, For
fac - tion - al zeal, In - cul - cat - ing al - ways a char - i - ty broad, For
one broth - er - hood; With san-dals fra - ter - nal their feet al - ways shod, For
len - ni - al day, The Lord's gold-en rule as the sym - bol - ic rod, For

they shall be call - ed the chil-dren of God, For they shall be call - ed the children of God.
they shall be call - ed the chil-dren of God, For they shall be call - ed the children of God.
they shall be call - ed the chil-dren of God, For they shall be call - ed the children of God.
they shall be call - ed the chil-dren of God, For they shall be call - ed the children of God.

Copyright, 1884, by Fillmore Bros. By permission.

192. Hungering and Thirsting.

Mat. 5: 6.

D. R. L.   J. H. F.

1. Hung'ring and thirsting ones, Right-eous-ness crav-ing, Who would on Je-sus as the rock seek to build, Look on the en-sign high Val-iant-ly wav-ing; Bless-ed are ye, for ye all shall be filled, Bless-ed are ye, for ye all shall be filled.
2. Seek-ing the Bread of Heav'n, Bread nev-er fail-ing, Com-ing like man-na, free of old, as God will'd, Take thou the prom-ise giv'n, Vic-to-ry hail-ing; Bless-ed are ye, for ye all shall be filled, Bless-ed are ye, for ye all shall be filled.
3. Seek ye the foun-tain pure, Seek liv-ing wa-ters, Flow-ing from prom-i-ses of Je-sus dis-tilled; Doubt not His pur-pos-es, Gra-cious and ho-ly; Bless-ed are ye, for ye all shall be filled, Bless-ed are ye, for ye all shall be filled.

Copyright, 1884, by Fillmore Bros. By permission.

193 Bringing in the Sheaves.

"*The harvest is the end of the world.*" — MATT. 13: 39.

KNOWLES SHAW. GEORGE A. MINOR, by per.

1. Sow-ing in the morn-ing, sow-ing seeds of kind-ness, Sow-ing in the noon-tide
2. Sow-ing in the sun-shine, sow-ing in the shad-ows, Fear-ing nei-ther clouds nor

and the dew-y eve; Wait-ing for the har-vest, and the time of reap-ing,
win-ter's chill-ing breeze; By and by the har-vest, and the la-bor end-ed,

CHORUS.

We shall come re-joic-ing, bring-ing in the sheaves. Bring-ing in the sheaves,
We shall come re-joic-ing, bring-ing in the sheaves.

bring-ing in the sheaves, We shall come re-joic-ing, bring-ing in the sheaves;

Bringing in the sheaves, bringing in the sheaves, We shall come rejoicing, bringing in the sheaves.

Peace. L. M. Male Voices.

Arranged from HOLZINGER.

194

1
O Lord! where'er Thy people meet,
There they behold Thy mercy-seat;
Where'er they seek Thee, Thou art found,
And every place is hallowed ground.

2
For Thou, within no walls confined,
Inhabitest the humble mind;
Such ever bring Thee where they come,
And going, take Thee to their home.

3
Here we may prove the power of prayer
To strengthen faith and sweeten care;
To teach our faint desires to rise,
And bring all heaven before our eyes.

COWPER. *Alt.*

195

1
O God, whose presence glows in all,
Within, around us, and above!
Thy word we bless, Thy name we call
Whose word is Truth, whose name is Love.

2
That love its holy influence pour
To keep us meek, and make us free;
And throw its binding blessing more
Round each with all, and all with Thee.

3
Send down its angel to our side,
Send in its calm upon the breast;
For we would know no other guide;
And we can need no other rest.

FROTHINGHAM. *Abr.*

Brightness. L. M. Male Voices.

Arr. from Franz Abt.

196

1
O Life that maketh all things new,—
The blooming earth, the thoughts of men!
Our pilgrim feet, wet with thy dew,
In gladness hither turn again.

2
From hand to hand the greeting flows,
From eye to eye the signals run,
From heart to heart the bright hope glows;
The seekers of the Light are one.

3
One in the freedom of the truth,
One in the joy of paths untrod,
One in the heart's perennial youth,
One in the larger thought of God;—

4
The freer step, the fuller breath,
The wide horizon's grander view,
The sense of Life that knows no death,—
The Life that maketh all things new.
Samuel Longfellow. Alt.

197.

1
Press on, press on! ye sons of light,
Untiring in your holy fight,
Still treading each temptation down,
And battling for a brighter crown.

2
Press on, press on! still look in faith
To Him who conquereth sin and death:
Then shall ye hear His word, "Well done."
True to the last, press on, press on!
William Gaskell.

Galilee. C. M. Male Voices.

Arr. from KÜCKEN.

198

1
We may not climb the heavenly steeps
To bring the Lord Christ down;
In vain we search the lowest deeps,
For Him no depths can drown.

2
But warm, sweet, tender, even yet
A present help is He;
And faith has yet its Olivet,
And love its Galilee.

3
The healing of the seamless dress
Is by our beds of pain;
We touch Him in life's throng and press,
And we are whole again.

4
O Lord and Master of us all,
Whate'er our name or sign,
We own Thy sway, we hear Thy call,
We test our lives by Thine!

J. G. WHITTIER, *Abr.*

199

1
Whatever dims thy sense of truth,
Or stains thy purity,
Though light as breath of summer air,
Count it as sin to thee.

2
Preserve the tablet of thy thoughts
From every blemish free,
While the Redeemer's lowly faith
Its temple makes with thee.

3
And pray of God, that grace be given
To tread this narrow way:—
How dark soever it may seem,
It leads to cloudless day.

Victory. S. M. Male Voices.

Arr. from BECKER.

200

1
'T is God the Spirit leads
 In paths before unknown;
The work to be performed is ours,
 The strength is all His own.

2
Supported by His grace,
 We still pursue our way;
Assured that we shall reach the prize,
 Secure in endless day.

3
'T is He that works to will,
 'T is He that works to do;
His is the power by which we act,
 His be the glory too.

MONTGOMERY. *Alt.*

201

1
Servants of Christ, arise,
 And gird you for the toil.
The dew of promise from the skies
 Already cheers the soil.

2
Go where the sick recline,
 Where mourning hearts deplore;
And where the sons of sorrow pine,
 Dispense your hallowed lore.

3
So shall you share the wealth,
 That earth may ne'er despoil,
And the blest gospel's saving health
 Repay your arduous toil.

Mrs. LYDIA H. SIGOURNEY. *Abr.*

Hope. 6s. Male Voices.

Adapted from MENDELSSOHN.

202

1
What is thy birthright, man,
   Child of the perfect One!
What is thy Father's plan
   For His beloved son?

2
Thou art Truth's honest child,
   Sinless and pure of heart.
Treading, meek, undefiled
   In th'Master's steps apart.

3
Take then the charmèd rod;
   Thou art not error's thrall!
Thou hast the gift from God—
   Dominion over all.

KATHLEEN. *Alt. and Abr.*

203

1
If God is all in all,
   His children cannot fear.
See baseless evil fall,
   Knowing that God is here!

2
If God is all, in space
   No subtle error creeps.
We see Truth's glowing face,
   And Love that never sleeps.

3
Oh, Perfect and Divine!
   We hear Thy loving call.
And seek no earthly shrine
   But "crown Thee Lord of All."

KATHLEEN. *Alt. and Abr.*

Joy. 7s, 6s, D. Male Voices.

Arranged from BESCHNITT.

204

1
A glorious day is dawning,
  And o'er the waking earth
The heralds of the morning
  Are springing into birth.
In dark and hidden places
  There shines the blessèd light;
The beam of truth displaces
  The darkness of the night.

2
The advocates of error,
  Foresee the glorious morn,
And hear in shrinking terror,
  The watchword of reform.
It rings from hill and valley,
  It breaks oppression's chain,
A thousand freemen rally,
  And swell the mighty strain.

3
The watchword has been spoken,
  The light has broken forth,
Far shines the blessèd token
  Upon the startled earth.

To hearts and homes benighted
  The blessèd truth is given,
And peace and love, united,
  Point upward unto heaven.

205

1
I know no life divided,
  O Lord of life, from Thee;
In Thee is life provided
  For all mankind and me:
I know no death, O Father,
  Because I live in Thee;
Thy life it is which frees us
  From death eternally.

2
I fear no tribulation,
  Since, whatsoe'er it be,
It makes no separation
  Between my Lord and me.
Since Thou, my God and Teacher,
  Vouchsafe to be my own,
Though poor, I shall be richer
  Than monarch on his throne.

REV. CARL JOHANN PHILIPP SPITTA.
Tr. by RICHARD MASSIE. *Alt. and Abr.*

Patience. 7s, (or 8s, 7s.) Male Voices.

Arranged from FRANZ ABT.

206

1
Wait, my heart, upon the Lord,
 To His gracious promise flee,
Laying hold upon His word.
 "As thy days thy strength shall be."

2
If the sorrows of thy case
 Seem peculiar still to thee,
God has promised needful grace—
 "As thy days thy strength shall be."

3
Rock of Ages, I'm secure,
 With Thy promise full and free ;
Faithful, positive, and sure—
 "As thy days thy strength shall be."

W. F. LLOYD. *Alt. and Abr.*

207

1
Know, O child, thy full salvation ;
 Rise o'er sin and fear and care ;
Joy to find, in every station,
 Something still to do, or bear.

2
Think what spirit dwells within thee ;
 Think what Father's smiles are thine ;
Think what Jesus did to win thee ;
 Child of heaven, canst thou repine ?

3
Haste thee on from grace to glory,
 Arm'd with faith and wing'd with pray'r,
Heav'n's eternal day before thee,
 God's own hand shall guide thee there.

HENRY FRANCIS LYTE. *Alt. and Abr.*

Courage. 8s & 7s. Male Voices.

MENDELSSOHN.

208

1
Onward, Christian, though the region
  Where thou art be drear and lone;
God hath set a guardian legion
  Very near thee,— press thou on!

2
By the thorn-road, and none other,
  Is the mount of vision won;
Tread it without shrinking, brother!
  Jesus trod it,— press thou on!

3
By thy trustful, calm endeavor,
  Guiding, cheering, like the sun,
Earth-bound hearts thou shalt deliver;
  Oh, for their sake, press thou on!

S. JOHNSON. *Abr.*

209

1
God is love; His mercy brightens
  All the path in which we rove;
Bliss He wakes and woe He lightens;
  God is wisdom, God is love.

2
E'en the hour that darkest seemeth,
  Will His changeless goodness prove;
From the gloom His brightness streameth,
  God is wisdom, God is love.

3
He with earthly cares entwineth
  Hope and comfort from above:
Everywhere His glory shineth;
  God is wisdom, God is love.

BOWRING. *Abr.*

Safety. 9s, 8s. Male Voices.

MENDELSSOHN.

210

1
In Thee, oh Spirit, true and tender,
  I find my Life, as God's own child;
Within Thy Light of glorious splendor,
  I lose the earth-clouds, drear and wild.

2
Within Thy Love is safe abiding
  From every thought that giveth fear;
Within Thy Truth, a perfect chiding,
  Should I forget that Thou art near.

3
In Thee I have no pain or sorrow,
  No anxious thought, no load of care.
Thou art the same to-day, to-morrow;
  Thy Love and Truth are everywhere.

F. A. F. *Abr.*

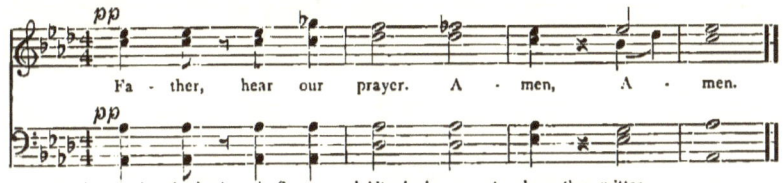

* May be sung by mixed voices, the Soprano and Alto singing one octave lower than written.

Gloria Patri. No. 1. For Male Voices.

L. B.

Glory be to the Father, and to the Son, And to the Ho-ly Ghost;

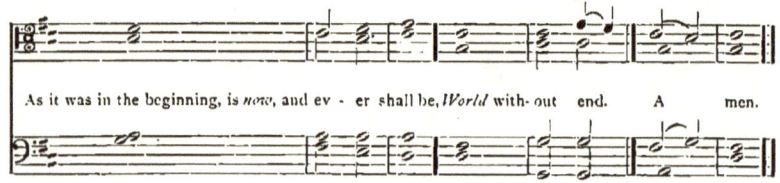

As it was in the beginning, is *now*, and ev - er shall be, *World* with- out end. A men.

Gloria Patri. No. 2. For Male Voices.

L. B.

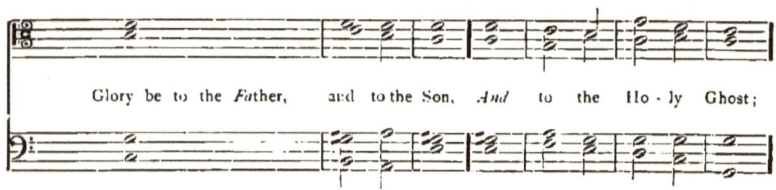

Glory be to the Father, and to the Son, And to the Ho-ly Ghost;

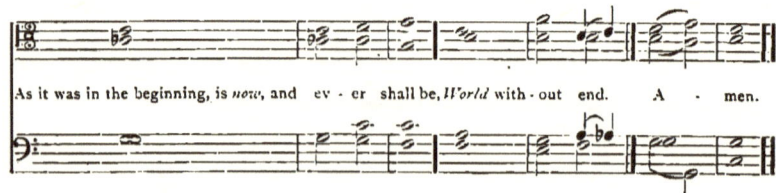

As it was in the beginning, is *now*, and ev - er shall be, *World* with - out end. A - men.

Gloria Patri. No. 3. For Mixed Voices.

Arr. from LANGDON.

Glory be to the *Father*, and to the Son, *And* to the Ho - ly Ghost;

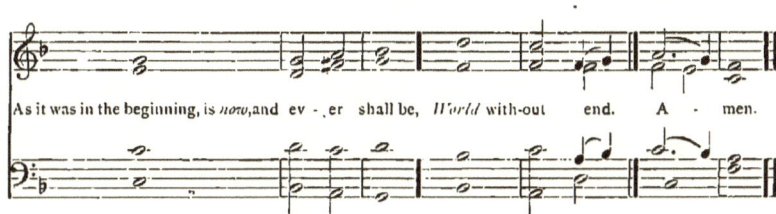

As it was in the beginning, is *now*, and ev - er shall be, *World* with-out end. A - men.

Gloria Patri. No. 4. For Mixed Voices.

WILLIAM BOYCE, Mus. Doc.

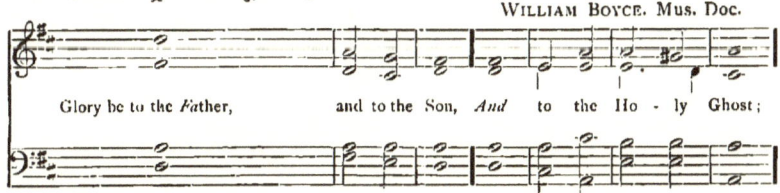

Glory be to the *Father*, and to the Son, *And* to the Ho - ly Ghost;

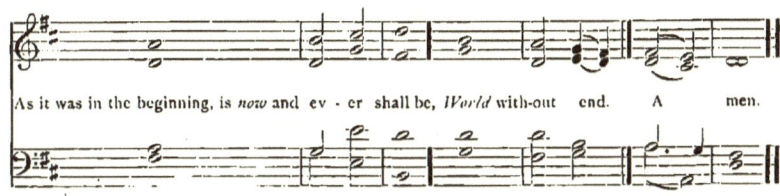

As it was in the beginning, is *now* and ev - er shall be, *World* with-out end. A men.

INDEX TO FIRST LINES

INDEX TO FIRST LINES.

	No.		No.
A glorious day is dawning	153, 204	God is love; His mercy brightens	114, 209
Abide not in the realm of dreams	18	God is my strong salvation	152
Abide with me: fast falls the eventide	165	God is the Life, the Truth, the Way	28
		God made all His creatures free	144
Be firm and be faithful, desert not the right	173	God's glory is a wondrous thing	45
Beneath the shadow of the cross	84	Gracious spirit, dwell with me	145
Beneath the thick but struggling cloud	58	Guide me, O Thou great Jehovah	134
Be true and list the voice within	37		
Blessed are those who thro' the flame	187	Had I the tongues of Greeks and Jews	14
Blessed the merciful	188	Happy the heart where graces reign	44
Blessed they in spirit poor	186	Happy the man who knows	109
Breaking through the clouds of darkness	127	Hath not thy heart within thee burned	16
Bright was the guiding star that led	80	Hear our prayer, oh gracious Father	117
		Heirs of unending life	104
Call the Lord thy sure salvation	112	Help us to help each other, Lord	53
Cast thy bread upon the waters	116	Here, O my Lord, I'd see Thee face to face	166
Christ for the world we sing	184	He that goeth forth with weeping	130
Church of the ever-living God	54	He that has God his guardian made	39
City of God, how broad and far	65	High in the heavens, eternal God	38
Come, thou all-transforming spirit	133	Holy Bible, book divine	142
Come to the land of peace	97	Holy Father, Thou hast taught us	129
Come, ye that know and fear the Lord	74	How beauteous on the mountains	151
		How beauteous were the works divine	23
Day by day the manna fell	135	How bless'd are they whose hearts are pure	51
		How firm a foundation, ye saints of the Lord	170
Eternal mind the Potter is	92	How gentle God's commands	93
Everlasting arms of love	136	How lovely are Thy dwellings, Lord	55
Every human tie may perish	132	How sweet, how heavenly is the sight	57
		How sweetly flowed the gospel sound	33
Faith grasps the blessing she desires	43	Hung'ring and thirsting ones	192
Father, hear the prayer we offer	120		
Father, my all in all Thou art	20	I am the Way, the Truth, the Life	41
Father, Thou joy of loving hearts	10	I cannot always trace the way	32
Fight the good fight with all thy might	13	I cannot walk in darkness long	78
From all that dwell below the skies	1	I know no life divided	154, 205
From out the hideous night	159	I look to Thee in every need	176
From the table now retiring	111	I praise Thee, Lord, for blessings sent	2
		I worship Thee, sweet Will of God	68
Gird thy heavenly armor on	162	If God is all in all	156, 203
God comes, with succor speedy	148	If my immortal Saviour lives	30

INDEX TO FIRST LINES.

	No.
If on our daily course, our mind	5
Immortal Love, forever full	77
Imposture shrinks from light	96
In atmosphere of love divine	81
In heavenly love abiding	149
In Thee, oh Spirit, true and tender	164, 210
It came upon the midnight clear	89
Jesus, what precept is like Thine	7
Joy to the world, the Lord is come	64
Kingdoms and thrones to God belong	6
Know, O child, thy full salvation	118, 207
Lead, kindly Light, amid the encircling gloom,	169
Let party names no more	98
Like wandering sheep o'er mountains cold	183
Look, ye saints! the day is breaking	131
Lord, I have made Thy word my choice	70
Lord, may Thy truth upon the heart	12
Lowly in heart to all who sought	87
Make channels for the streams of love	86
Make haste, O man, to do	110
Man is the noblest work of God	47
Mighty God, the First, the Last	137
My feet shall never slide	175
Nearer, my God, to Thee	158
Now is the time approaching	150
Now sweeping down the years untold	121
Now to our loving Father, God	59
O be not faithless! with the morn	177
O blessed are the pure in heart!	189
O blessed are they who are makers of peace	190
O for a faith that will not shrink	67
O God, whose presence glows in all	26, 195
O, he whom Jesus loved has truly spoken	172
O Love! O Life! Our faith and sight	71
O Lord, where'er Thy people meet	25, 194
O, my people, journeying onward	125
O pure Reformers! not in vain	83
O Thou great Friend to all the sons of men	168
Oh, do not bar your mind	107
Oh! ever on our earthly path	52
Oh Life, that maketh all things new	3, 196
Oh, Lord, I would delight in Thee	91
Oh, Love Divine, whose constant beam	34

	No.
Oh, not alone with outward sign	90
Oh, sometimes gleams upon our sight	17
Oh, speed thee, Christian, on thy way	56
Oh Spirit, source of light	95
O'er waiting harpstrings of the mind	163
One cup of healing oil and wine	35
One holy Church of God appears	85
On the night of that last supper	119
Onward, Christian Soldiers	157
Onward, Christian, though the region	113, 208
On what are you building, my brother?	180
Our God is love; and all His saints	73
Our God shall reign where'er the sun	9
Our heaven is everywhere	94
Out of sadness into gladness	179
Partners of a glorious hope	138
Peace be to this congregation	128
Planted in Christ, the living vine	66
Prayer is the heart's sincere desire	88
Press on, dear traveller, press on	40
Press on, press on, ye sons of light	4, 197
Rouse, ye soldiers of the cross	185
Saw ye my Saviour? Heard ye the glad sound.	178
Say, is your lamp burning, my brother?	191
Scorn not the slightest word or deed	48
Servants of Christ, arise	102, 201
Shepherd, show me how to go	161
Soldiers of Christ, arise	103
Sowing in the morning	193
Sow in the morn thy seed	108
Speak gently, it is better far	60
Still, still with Thee, when purple morning breaketh	171
Sun of our life, Thy quickening ray	8
Supreme in wisdom as in power	61
Take up thy cross, the Saviour said	27
Teach me, my God and King	100
The Christian warrior, see him stand	31
The God who made both heaven and earth	79
The hopes Thy holy word supplies	22
The lifted eye and bended knee	36
The light of the world you must be	181
The loving Friend to all who bowed	82
The morning light is breaking	147
The Spirit breathes upon the word	42

INDEX TO FIRST LINES.

	No.
Theories which thousands cherish	123
They are slaves who will not choose	143
They who seek the throne of grace	141
Thine is a living way	99
Thou art the Way, to Thee alone	75
Thy will, almighty Father, Thine	24
'T is God, the spirit leads	101, 200
To us a Child of Hope is born	69
True, the heart grows rich in giving	126
Truth comes alike to all	160
Upon the Gospel's sacred page	15
Vainly, through night's weary hours	124
Wait, my heart, upon the Lord	140, 206
Walk in the light! So thou shalt know	63
Walk with your God, along the road	76
Watchman, tell us of the night	146
We may not climb the heavenly steeps	49, 198

	No.
We say to all men far and near	46
We walk by faith of joys to come	72
Well for him who all things losing	115
Whatever dims thy sense of truth	50, 199
What is thy birthright, man	155, 202
When God is seen with men to dwell	21
When Jesus, our great master, came	29
When like a stranger on our sphere	19
While Thou, O my God, art my help and defender	174
Whoso heareth and doeth these sayings of mine	182
Why is thy faith, O child of God, so small?	167
Why search the future and the past	11
With Love and Peace and Joy supreme	122
Word of life, most pure, most strong	139
Ye messengers of Christ	106
Ye timid saints, fresh courage take	1, 62
Ye servants of the Lord	105

SELECTIONS FOR SUNDAY SCHOOL AND SPECIAL OCCASIONS.

	Page
Blessed are the merciful	205
Blessed are the peacemakers	207
Blessed are the persecuted	204
Blessed are the poor in spirit	203
Blessed are the pure in heart	206
Bringing in the sheaves	210
Christ for the world we sing	201
Hungering and thirsting	209

	Page
I am the way	200
Is your lamp burning?	208
Out of self and into Thee	195
Rouse ye, soldiers!	202
The Light of the world	197
The Rock and the Sand	196
These sayings of Mine	198

TUNES FOR MALE VOICES.

	Page
Brightness .... L. M.	212
Courage 8s, 7s	218
Galilee .... C. M.	213
Hope 6s	215
Joy .... 7s, 6s, D.	216
Patience .... 7s (or 8s, 7s)	217
Peace .... L. M.	211
Safety 9s, 8s	219
Victory .... S. M.	214

RESPONSES.
FOR MALE (OR MIXED) VOICES.

	Page
Father, hear our prayer .... (No. 1)	220
Father, hear our prayer .... (No. 4)	220
Father, O hear us .... (No. 3)	220
Hear us when we pray to Thee. (No. 2)	220

CHANTS.

Gloria Patri.	(No. 1.) Male voices	221
Gloria Patri.	(No. 2.) Male voices	221
Gloria Patri.	(No. 3.) Mixed voices	222
Gloria Patri.	(No. 4.) Mixed voices	222

METRICAL INDEX

METRICAL INDEX.

L. M.

TUNE	AUTHOR	PAGE
ALL SAINTS,	Knapp,	12
Second Tune,	German,	13
Third Tune,	Brackett,	13
DUKE STREET,	Hatton,	28
Second Tune,	Tours,	29
Third Tune,	Brackett,	29
FEDERAL STREET,	Oliver,	24
Second Tune,	Wesley,	25
Third Tune,	Brackett,	25
GERMANY,	Beethoven,	8
Second Tune,	Smart,	9
Third Tune,	Brackett,	9
HAMBURG,	Arr. by Mason,	30
Second Tune,	Old Melody,	31
Third Tune,	Brackett,	31
HEBRON,	Mason,	32
Second Tune,	Barnby,	33
Third Tune,	Brackett,	33
HURSLEY,	Haydn—Monk,	26
Second Tune,	Schumann,	27
Third Tune,	Brackett,	27
LINWOOD,	Rossini,	38
Second Tune,	Hodges,	39
Third Tune,	Brackett,	39
MISSIONARY CHANT,	Zeuner,	4
Second Tune,	Monk,	5
Third Tune,	Brackett,	5
OLD HUNDRED,	Franck,	2
Second Tune,	Ancient,	3
Third Tune,	Brackett,	3
PARK STREET,	Venua,	14
Second Tune,	Tuxton,	15
Third Tune,	Brackett,	15
RETREAT,	Hastings,	20
Second Tune,	Ancient German,	21
Third Tune,	Brackett,	21
ROCKINGHAM,	Mason,	36
Second Tune,	Garrett,	37
Third Tune,	Brackett,	37

TUNE	AUTHOR	PAGE
TRURO,	Burney,	6
Second Tune,	Webb,	7
Third Tune,	Brackett,	7
WARD,	Arr. by Mason,	34
Second Tune,	Miller,	35
Third Tune,	Brackett,	35
WARE,	Kingsley,	10
Second Tune,	Ancient,	11
Third Tune,	Brackett,	11
WAREHAM,	Knapp,	22
Second Tune,	Old Melody,	23
Third Tune,	Brackett,	23
WOODWORTH,	Bradbury,	18
Second Tune,	Ancient German,	19
Third Tune,	Brackett,	19
ZEPHYR,	Bradbury,	16
Second Tune,	Dykes,	17
Third Tune,	Brackett,	17

L. M. 6 lines.

TUNE	AUTHOR	PAGE
BERA,	Gould,	40
Second Tune,	Monk,	41
Third Tune,	Brackett,	41

C. M.

TUNE	AUTHOR	PAGE
ARLINGTON,	Arne,	50
Second Tune,	Gauntlett,	51
Third Tune,	Brackett,	51
AVON,	Wilson,	74
Second Tune,	Sangster,	75
Third Tune,	Brackett,	75
AZMON,	Arr. by Mason,	62
Second Tune,	Foster,	93
Third Tune,	Brackett,	63
BALERMA,	Wilson,	58
Second Tune,	Richardson,	59
Third Tune,	Brackett,	59
BELMONT,	Mozart,	68
Second Tune,	Smart,	69
Third Tune,	Brackett,	69

METRICAL INDEX.

C. M.—Continued.

TUNE	AUTHOR	PAGE
CHRISTMAS,	Handel,	70
Second Tune,	From Day's Psalter,	71
Third Tune,	Brackett,	71
COLCHESTER,	Purcell,	78
Second Tune,	Hervey,	79
Third Tune,	Brackett,	79
CORONATION,	Holden,	46
Second Tune,	Novello,	47
Third Tune,	Brackett,	47
COVENTRY,	English Melody,	80
Second Tune,	Smith,	81
Third Tune,	Brackett,	81
DEDHAM,	Gardiner,	44
Second Tune,	Comley,	45
Third Tune,	Brackett,	45
DUNDEE,	Franc,	84
Second Tune,	Irons,	85
Third Tune,	Brackett,	85
ECKHARDTSHEIM,	Zeuner,	88
Second Tune,	Dykes,	89
Third Tune,	Brackett,	89
EVAN,	Havergal,	60
Second Tune,	Roberts,	61
Third Tune,	Brackett,	61
HEBER,	Kingsley,	76
Second Tune,	Lahee,	77
Third Tune,	Brackett,	77
MAITLAND,	Allen,	56
Second Tune,	Stainer,	57
Third Tune,	Brackett,	57
MANOAH,	Rossini,	52
Second Tune,	Reinagle,	53
Third Tune,	Brackett,	53
NAOMI,	Naegeli—Mason,	54
Second Tune,	Hopkins,	55
Third Tune,	Brackett,	55
OAKSVILLE,	Zeuner,	48
Second Tune,	Hopkins,	49
Third Tune,	Brackett,	49
ORTONVILLE,	Hastings,	42
Second Tune,	Baker—Monk,	43
Third Tune,	Brackett,	43

TUNE	AUTHOR	PAGE
PETERBOROUGH,	Harrison,	64
Second Tune,	Wright,	65
Third Tune,	Brackett,	65
SIMPSON,	Spohr,	72
Second Tune,	Turpin,	73
Third Tune,	Brackett,	73
SOUTHPORT,	Kingsley,	82
Second Tune,	Denby,	83
Third Tune,	Brackett,	83
ST. AGNES,	Dykes,	66
Second Tune,	Ravenscroft,	67
Third Tune,	Brackett,	67
ST. MARTIN'S,	Tansur,	86
Second Tune,	Hoyte,	87
Third Tune,	Brackett,	87

C. M. D.

TUNE	AUTHOR	PAGE
BRATTLE STREET,	Pleyel,	92
Second Tune,	Spohr,	93
Third Tune,	Brackett,	93
ST. ASAPH,	Giornovichi,	90
Second Tune,	Sullivan,	91
Third Tune,	Brackett,	91

S. M.

TUNE	AUTHOR	PAGE
ATHOL,	Harrison,	106
Second Tune, from Kölner Gesangbuch,		107
Third Tune,	Brackett,	107
BOYLSTON,	Lowell Mason,	104
Second Tune,	Oakeley,	105
Third Tune,	Brackett,	105
DENNIS,	Arr. by Mason,	94
Second Tune,	Hopkins,	95
Third Tune,	Brackett,	95
LABAN,	Lowell Mason,	100
Second Tune,	Watson,	101
Third Tune,	Brackett,	101
OLMUTZ,	Arr. by Mason,	108
Second Tune, from Müller's Choralbuch,		109
Third Tune,	Brackett,	109
SILVER STREET,	Smith,	110
Second Tune,	Anon.,	111
Third Tune,	Brackett,	111
STATE STREET,	Woodman,	98
Second Tune,	Monk,	99
Third Tune,	Brackett,	99

METRICAL INDEX.

S. M.—Continued.

TUNE	AUTHOR	PAGE
ST. THOMAS,	Tansur,	102
Second Tune,	Gauntlett,	103
Third Tune,	Brackett,	103
THATCHER,	Handel,	96
Second Tune,	Stainer,	97
Third Tune,	Brackett,	97

6s.

ST. CECILIA,	Hayne,	158
Second Tune,	Smart,	159
Third Tune,	Brackett,	159

6s, 5s.

ST. GERTRUDE,	Sullivan,	160
Second Tune,	Haydn — Dykes,	161
Third Tune,	Brackett,	161

6s, 4s.

BETHANY,	Mason,	162
Second Tune,	Dykes,	163
Third Tune,	Brackett,	163
ITALIAN HYMN,	Giardini,	164
Second Tune,	Dykes,	165
Third Tune,	Brackett,	165

7s.

DIJON,	German Evening Hymn,	142
Second Tune,	Dykes,	143
Third Tune,	Brackett,	143
HENDON,	Malan,	138
Second Tune,	Gauntlett,	139
Third Tune,	Brackett,	139
HERFORD,	English Tune,	144
Second Tune,	Foster,	145
Third Tune,	Brackett,	145
NUREMBERG,	Ahle,	136
Second Tune,	Knecht,	137
Third Tune,	Brackett,	137
PLEYEL,	Pleyel, .	140
Second Tune,	Stainer,	141
Third Tune,	Brackett,	141

7s, 6 Lines.

HALLE,	Haydn,	146
Second Tune,	Smart,	147
Third Tune,	Brackett,	147

7s, D.

TUNE	AUTHOR	PAGE
WATCHMAN,	Mason,	148
Second Tune,	Elvey,	149
Third Tune,	Brackett,	149

7, 7, 7, 3.

VESPER,	Stainer,	168
Second Tune,	Barnby,	169
Third Tune,	Brackett,	169

7s, 6s, D.

EWING,	Ewing,	152
Second Tune,	Elliott,	153
Third Tune,	Brackett,	153
GREENLAND,	From Lausane Psalter,	154
Second Tune,	Stainer,	155
Third Tune,	Brackett,	155
MISSIONARY HYMN,	Mason,	156
Second Tune,	Monk,	157
Third Tune,	Brackett,	157
WEBB,	Webb,	150
Second Tune,	Wesley,	151
Third Tune,	Brackett,	151

7s, 5s, D.

ST. NICOLAS,	Hoyte,	166
Second Tune,	MacFarren,	167
Third Tune,	Brackett,	167

8s, 7s.

BARTIMEUS,	Jenks,	114
Second Tune,	Bach — Steggall,	115
Third Tune,	Brackett,	115
RATHBUN,	Conkey,	116
Second Tune,	Monk,	117
Third Tune,	Brackett,	117
SCIENCE,	Brackett,	122
Second Tune,	Dykes,	123
Third Tune,	Brackett,	123
SICILY,	Sicilian Melody,	112
Second Tune,	Dykes,	113
Third Tune,	Brackett,	113

METRICAL INDEX.

8s, 7s.—Continued.

TUNE	AUTHOR	PAGE
STOCKWELL,	Jones,	118
Second Tune,	Redhead,	119
Third Tune,	Brackett,	119
ST. SYLVESTER,	Dykes,	124
Second Tune,	Neander,	125
Third Tune,	Brackett,	125
WILMOT,	Weber,	120
Second Tune, from Gothäer Cantional,		121
Third Tune,	Brackett,	121

8s, 7s, D.

TUNE	AUTHOR	PAGE
AUTUMN,	Marechio,	126
Second Tune,	Haydn,	127
Third Tune,	Brackett,	127
BAVARIA,	German,	128
Second Tune,	Smart,	129
Third Tune,	Brackett,	129
GREENVILLE,	Rousseau,	130
Second Tune,	Lloyd,	131
Third Tune,	Brackett,	131

8s, 7s, 4s.

TUNE	AUTHOR	PAGE
WEIMAR,	Ancient Melody,	132
Second Tune,	Monk,	133
Third Tune,	Brackett,	133
ZION,	Hastings,	134
Second Tune,	Irons,	135
Third Tune,	Brackett,	135

8, 6, 8, 6, 8, 8.

TUNE	AUTHOR	PAGE
CALM,	Hastings,	192
Second Tune,	Hopkins,	193
Third Tune,	Brackett,	193

8s, 4s.

TUNE	AUTHOR	PAGE
EDDY,	Brackett,	170
Second Tune,	Monk,	171
Third Tune,	Brackett,	171

9s, 8s.

TUNE	AUTHOR	PAGE
ST. VINCENT,	Uglow,	172
Second Tune,	Hodges,	173
Third Tune,	Brackett,	173

10s.

TUNE	AUTHOR	PAGE
BERLIN,	Mendelssohn,	178
Second Tune,	Monk,	179
Third Tune,	Brackett,	179
EVENTIDE,	Monk,	174
Second Tune,	Smart,	175
Third Tune,	Brackett,	175
REDEMPTOR,	Brown,	176
Second Tune,	Monk,	177
Third Tune,	Brackett,	177
TRUTH,	Pleyel,	180
Second Tune,	Hulton,	181
Third Tune,	Brackett,	181

10, 7, 7, 7, 9.

TUNE	AUTHOR	PAGE
COMMUNION HYMN,	Brackett,	194

10, 4, 10, 4, 10, 10.

TUNE	AUTHOR	PAGE
LUX BENIGNA,	Dykes,	182
Second Tune,	Wainwright,	183
Third Tune,	Brackett,	183

11s.

TUNE	AUTHOR	PAGE
LYONS,	Haydn,	188
Second Tune,	Stephens,	189
Third Tune,	Brackett,	189
PORTUGUESE HYMN,	Reading,	184
Second Tune,	Barnby,	185
Third Tune,	Brackett,	185

11s, 10s.

TUNE	AUTHOR	PAGE
HENLEY,	Mason,	186
Second Tune,	Dykes,	187
Third Tune,	Brackett,	187

12s, 11s.

TUNE	AUTHOR	PAGE
LYONS,	Haydn,	188
Second Tune,	Stephens,	189
Third Tune,	Brackett,	189

H. M.

TUNE	AUTHOR	PAGE
LISCHER,	Schneider,	190
Second Tune,	Stainer,	191
Third Tune,	Brackett,	191

www.ingramcontent.com/pod-product-compliance
Lightning Source LLC
Chambersburg PA
CBHW021807230426
43669CB00008B/663